STOCK MA

INVESTING

A Crash Course Guide to Trading from

Beginners to Expert:

How to Create Passive Income to Get

Fresh Money to Buy and Sell Options

Anthony Sinclair

2

Table of Contents

6

Introduction

The fact is that for most young people, investing might not be the most important thing in their lives. Until they get older and established in a career, saving and investing for retirement may not be at the top of their priority list; there are other things that might seem more pressing and exciting at this stage in life.

When you're young, you have limited resources to invest. You're also still trying to figure out who you are — what kind of career or education you want to pursue, and how much risk you want to take with your money. For these reasons, it's not a good idea to jump into the stock market before you have a better handle on your financial circumstances and goals.

This doesn't mean you'll never be able to invest in the stock market, but it does mean that you're a long way off from making a decision that will have a major impact on your life. Until then, there are plenty of other ways to get started with investing and he stock market without getting ahead of yourself.

It is difficult to believe there was a time when the stock market didn't exist. The stock market is on the tip of nearly everyone's tongue. Even individuals who do not invest at least know it exists. It is largely understood that the New York Stock Exchange is the biggest market of them all, with any company listed on it that wants to be recognized globally. However, how did the stock market come to fruition? Is there more than the NYSE (New York Stock Exchange)? There are more exchanges and it started with the Real Merchants of Venice and British Coffeehouses.

Europe was filled with moneylenders that filled in the gaps of the larger banks. Moneylenders would trade between themselves. One lender might get rid of a high-risk, high-interest loan by trading it to another lender. Moneylenders also purchased government debt. In a natural evolution, lenders started selling debts to customers who were looking to invest.

Investors also put their money into ships and crews. Most of the time-limited liability companies would go on a single voyage to gain merchandise from Asia and the East Indies as a way to bring a profit to the investor. New companies were usually formed for the next voyage to reduce the risk of investing in ships that could end up in disaster. The East India companies worked with investors by providing dividends made from the goods that came in. Stocks were now in place, where the first joint-stock company was created. At the time, there were royal charters that made competition impossible and thus, investors gained huge profits.

It was not without its troubles. The stock market is based on economic stability. When instability reigns the stock market can crash because there is no liquidity, which is what happened during the Great Depression. Everyone saw the banks failing due to debts and little liquidity, which in turn caused others to suffer, businesses too close, and stock shares to plummet.

The stock market formed from a need to have a place to conduct the business of selling shares, which was already happening. Governments needed to regulate stock sales, and prevent issues like the SSC crash. Nevertheless, there was also greed on behalf of wealthy citizens. There was a clear way to earn money from someone else's labor, thus the stock exchanges were started.

Investors and traders sell stocks after the IPO based on the perceived value. A company's value can go up or down, which is where investors make their money. A company's stock price that rises can provide a profit. If an investor has purchased those shares and the price or company value decreases, then the investor will lose money. In addition, the investors and traders will push the price in an up or down direction.

Investors have one of two goals: investing in the short or the long term. A long-term investment is based on a stock continuing to rise in price. A short-term investment is to gain quick cash and pulling out before the stock price decreases.

Mature companies offer dividends to their shareholders. If you have stocks, then you are a shareholder in a company. If you hold the stocks long enough and have enough stock in a company, you can vote on new board members. Dividends are company profits that you get a cut of.

Investors will make money on the price fluctuations and the dividends. A seller is often trying to gain a profit by selling to a new buyer. The new buyer is also trying to buy as low as possible so that when the stock price continues to increase, they will make a profit.

The profit is calculated by taking the initial buy price and subtracting it from the closing or sale price. For example, if you buy into Google at $400 and wait for it to go up to $600, then the profit is $200 per share.

Sellers can push the price down due to supply and demand. This financial market works based on supply and demand.

You should already know that in economics when there is an oversupply of a product, the price is low. There is no demand for the product; therefore, a company or in this case a stock is not of interest.

When there is an undersupply of something like a stock, the demand is high. With more interested parties, the price will continue to increase.

If there is an even amount of supply and demand, then equality exists and there is no movement to see.

For the stock market, when too many people sell a stock, the price will decline. When too many people buy a stock, the price will continue to rise. If there is an equal number of shares and interest, then the price usually trades sideways because there is a balance.

As you learn about the stock market, you will hear the word volume, often. Volume is the number of shares that change hands on a daily basis. Millions of shares can be traded on the stock exchange in a day as investors attempt to make money from increasing or decreasing prices.

The stock market works based on the interest or volume of traders. If a stock does not have any volume or very little, then it is not being actively traded, thus the price is not moving. Traders such as market makers get into the market in order to buy or sell stocks for companies with low volume. They do not stop a stock from rising or falling. Instead, market makers just trying to garner interest in the company's stock.

When it comes to the stock market and traders, most individuals are looking for high-volume traders, with fluctuating prices. They get in, make a profit, and get out finding the next big profit.

BEGINNERS

Chapter 1. The Basics of Investing in Stocks

Delayed gratification is a strong suit that few have and this is why investing has always been a challenge for many. You want to make money but not in a decade or a couple of years, but right now. Ponzi schemes aside, profitable investments that can actually build you wealth for a lifetime take time and lots of patience. These two things are probably the most important tools that any beginner in stock market investing needs to be aware of.

Our motivations for investing may differ but ultimately all investments have one goal in common; to make a return or profit on the investment. You may be eyeing early retirement, you may be in it for financial freedom or maybe you are just sick of having your money sitting in a savings account attracting point nothing interest. Regardless of what your goals are, the idea behind investing is that you use your money to make more money.

The stock market presents a unique opportunity for both retail and corporate investors because anyone can do it at any scale. You can invest as little as $1000 or as much as a million dollars. There are room and opportunity for everyone to get in and make a decent return on their investment. That said, the stock market is not the way to go if you want quick money. Stocks like most other investments have one thing in common; they depend on the power of time.

Time is your biggest ally when it comes to investing. If you have been waiting for a magical moment when you will have "enough" money to start investing, the bad news is that you will probably never have "enough" money and the other bad news is that the right time to start investing was yesterday.

A common misconception that most people have is that you need to have a lot of money to start investing. In actual fact, people who invest do not necessarily have more money than you, they simply make investing a priority. And because they make investing a priority, they end up having more money than you. See how that works?

Unlike consumption, investment takes money out of your pocket and puts it towards your future. When you can think of investment as an insurance policy to safeguard your financial future then the decision on when and if to invest becomes pretty much a no-brainer. Nobody wants to be cash-strapped forever or have to work themselves to the grave because they did not put their money to work when they had the chance.

The beauty of this golden age of technology that we live in is that anyone with the will and determination to do so can access all the tools they need to start investing in the stock market. This ease of accessibility coupled with its affordability has made the stock market increasingly popular with retail investors. With just a few a hundred dollars you can find an online brokerage at the click of a button and get started as an investor in the stock market. Yes, it is that easy. Before you jump on the bandwagon, however, it is important to understand what you are investing in. The natural starting point is, of course, understanding how the stock market works.

How Does the Stock Market Work?

It is no coincidence that most people who have wealth have a big part of this wealth invested in stocks. Stocks carry their fair share of risks for any investor but when done right, stock market investing can be one of the most efficient ways to build and retain wealth.

A stock market is an exchange where people trade by buying and selling shares on traded companies. Once you have bought shares in a company your stock gives you ownership of a small part of that company. With this ownership, the value of your investment will be determined by the movements of the price of the company's shares. If for instance, you bought Apple stocks and the price moves up while you are holding the stock then the value of your investment increases. On the other hand, if the price of the Apple stocks decreases while you are holding the stocks, the value of your investment decreases.

The price of a stock is driven by the forces of supply and demand. Naturally, when the demand for a particular stock is higher than the supply, the price of that stock will increase. In much the same way, when the supply is higher than the demand, then the price of that stock will decrease. In essence, the stock price is a reflection of the value as set by the market conditions. When you buy a stock as an investor, your general goal is to make money when the price of the stock increases. This is why a big part of investing in the stock market is knowing how to select the right stocks to buy.

When the price of the shares you have appreciates, you can sell your shares at a profit. This means that you will get a return on your investment and you can reinvest your capital back into the market or you can cash out. The beauty of stock market investing is that there is usually no limit to how long you can hold your investment. You can keep your shares for 20 years or you can choose to sell them when the share price appreciates. This will ultimately depend on what your end goal is.

Price appreciation is not the only way to make money in the stock market. Dividends are payments made out to shareholders when a company makes a profit. This means that depending on the type of shares you have, you will receive dividends from the company whose shares you hold.

For instance, if you bought Tesla stocks and the company pays out dividends quarterly to their shareholders, you will get a percentage of these dividends based on the value of your shares. You can choose to take these dividends as a cash payment or you can choose to reinvest them back into the company by buying more shares.

It is important to note that not all companies pay dividends. This means that if you want to make money in the stock market by earning regular dividends, you will need to understand the type of stocks to buy and which company's stocks will get you dividends.

Stock exchanges like the NYSE (New York Stock Exchange), NASDAQ, the Tokyo Stock Exchange are some of the largest exchanges. However, stocks are also sold in over-the-counter markets where they trade directly through brokers and not in open exchanges like the NYSE. These markets are referred to as secondary markets where investors trade stocks by buying and selling amongst themselves.

Basic Terms and Concepts

- **Stocks**

   A stock is a share of ownership in a company. Stocks are also referred to as shares. When you buy a stock you acquire a fraction of ownership of the company whose shares you have bought. When you buy stocks, you become a shareholder in a particular company and the percentage or size of your shares will determine the dividends you can earn.

Investors in the stock market can make money from their stocks in different ways. You can earn money in the form of dividends paid out on the shares you own. You can also earn money by selling your shares or stocks.

- **Common Stock**

Common stocks give you ownership of a company based on the number of shares you own. Common stocks are the most basic type of shares to own and they entitle you to dividends where applicable and voting rates proportionate to the shares you own.

- **Preferred Stock**

Preferred stocks entitle you to a fixed dividend rate for your shares. With this type of stock, you earn dividends before shareholders who have common stock but you do not get voting rights. Unlike shareholders of common stocks, preferred stocks give you a guarantee that you will receive dividends on your stock.

- **Penny Stocks**

A penny stock is a stock that trades for less than $5 per share. Penny stocks are typically short-term holdings where you want to take advantage of price movements in volatile markets. Penny stocks investing works for short-term investors who do not plan to hold the stocks for long periods.

- **Blue Chip Stocks**

Blue-chip stocks are shares of large established corporations that have solid reputations in the market. Blue-chip stocks are characterized by solid balance sheets and steady cash flows. Most blue-chip stocks have a history of earning increasing dividends for their shareholders. These types of stocks are ideal for long-term investors who want to hold stocks for long periods.

- **Primary Market**

   In a primary market, companies sell their shares directly to investors. In most cases, companies in primary markets sell to corporations and institutions rather than to individual investors. Hedge funds, mutual funds, and similar investors are typically the kind of investors that buy shares directly from companies in primary markets.

- **Secondary Markets**

   In a secondary market, investors buy and sell shares amongst themselves. Individual investors buy shares in secondary markets. In this type of market, you can choose to buy shares of a particular company or a mix of different companies' shares in exchange-traded funds or EFTs.

- **Over-the-Counter Markets**

  OTC markets are where companies that are not listed in exchanges like NYSE trade their shares. In OTC markets there is no public price for the shares and the value of the transaction is dependent on the buyer and seller.

- **Bid**

  A bid is a price at which you want to buy the share.

- **Ask**

  The ask is the price at which the seller wants to sell the share at

- **Spread**

  The spread is the difference between the bids and sell prices of a stock. If you want to buy a stock at $50 and the buyer wants to sell it at $45, the spread, in this case, is $5.

- **Volatility**

  Volatility refers to the movement of share prices in the market. When the price fluctuates widely within short periods of time then it is said to be highly volatile. The higher the volatility of a particular share, the higher the risk associated with it and also the higher the profit potential.

- **Dividend**

  A dividend is the percentage of a company's earnings that is paid out to shareholders. Dividends can be paid out annually or quarterly depending on the company. Not all companies pay dividends to the shareholders.

- **Broker**

  A broker is a trader who buys and sells shares for an investor for a fee or commission.

- **Bear Market**

  A bear market refers to a downward trend in the market where stock prices are falling

- **Bull Market**

  A bull market refers to an upward trend in the market where stock prices are rising.

- **Beta**

  Beta is the measurement of the price of a stock relative to the movement of the whole market. If a stock moves 1.5 points for every 1-point move in the market, then it has a beta of 1.5.

- **Index**

  An index is a measure that is used as a benchmark to gauge market performance. Some of the most famous indices include the Dow Jones and the S&P 500.

Chapter 2. Steps to Evaluate Your Financial Health, Setting, Goals (What to Consider Before Opening a New Account)

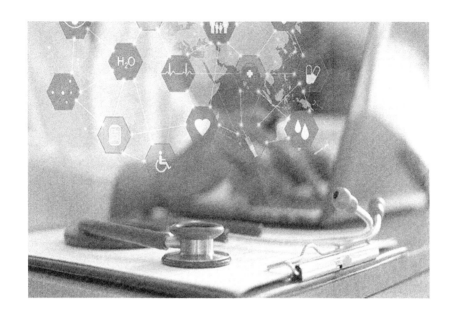

There are many ways to go about investing and knowing which path to take can be a daunting process. You can narrow down the possibilities to a strategy that works for you by evaluating your current financial situation. This should be done before you enter into your first trade. To be successful, an investor needs a clear picture of where they are going. Keep in mind this is not a one-time event. You should reevaluate your financial situation on an annual basis since it's going to be changing. When you find yourself in a different financial situation, your investment strategies will change over time.

Where

Establishing a starting point is the first step. You don't have to be a financial wizard, but you need to be aware of your present situation before jumping in and buying stocks. Consider the following scenario. An investor with a large personal debt that has an interest rate of 17% keeps putting money in the stock market, hoping to build wealth over time. That sounds reasonable, but most market returns are, going to be in the range of 5-10%. That means that someone in this situation is actually losing money.

Seek Liquidity

We are going to recommend that you look for assets you can sell.

The money can be used to pay debts, back taxes, or to seed investment capital. You'll want to list all of your assets by liquidity, which means how easily they can be converted into cash. You'll also want to consider how much cash you can raise by selling each item if you were to sell it. A house might have a lot more value than a television set, but you might sell the television set in 24 hours while you'd have to wait months to sell the house.

Dealing with Debts

Taking care of debts is one of the first things that a budding investor needs to do. While you might be anxious to get started with a large-scale investment plan if you have debts to take care of you might want to put it off. So, the first step in preparing your investment plan is to create a simple balance sheet. You don't have to be an accountant, and you're only doing this for yourself, but it needs to be honest and accurate.

You're going to want to put together a listing of all of your assets and liabilities. When compiling assets, include everything of value that you could possibly sell. This could be a computer that you're not using, a dusty TV in a room nobody goes into very often, or an old guitar. Selling things, you don't need can help you pay off debts faster and raise investment capital. You might object that you wouldn't raise much money but imagine having an extra $500 to $1,000 to start off with.

When listing your liabilities, you're going to want to know how much debt you have, what the interest rates are, and what your monthly payments are.

Monthly payments are less important than interest rates. Once you've listed all of your debts, you'll want to develop a plan to pay them off in a reasonable amount of time. There are many calculators available online, and you can also read many books on how to pay off debt. The series of books by debt guru Dave Ramsey is highly recommended. Here is an example of a good debt calculator:

https://www.creditkarma.com/calculators/debt_repayment/

You can use this calculator to figure out how long it will take to pay off a debt for a given monthly payment. You can enter the interest rate, and the time frame you would like along with the monthly payment you're willing to make. Start off with the current minimum payment in order to determine the time required to pay off the debt and work up from there.

In this example, we considered a $21,000 debt with a high 11% interest rate. Paying $450 a month would take five years to pay off the debt.

Additional Debt Repayment Information

Full Payoff

Balance	Interest Rate	Expected Monthly Payment	Expected Payoff Time
$21,000	11%	$450	62 months

Debt Repayment Chart

Principal	$21,370
Interest	$6,530

Click on the chart to see how much interest you will pay over the life of the debt.

That isn't a good situation to be in — do you want to saddle yourself with a $21,000 debt for five years?

When you have listed all of your debts, then you can prioritize them. In order to make the most progress in the shortest amount of time, it can be helpful to tackle the smallest debts first. This not only helps you get rid of your debt faster, but it will also have psychological benefits as you improve your financial situation.

If you have back taxes, you should make these a priority. The reason is that the government tacks on lots of fees and penalties, and if the tax debt is allowed to sit around, it can grow substantially in size. Get payment plans arranged to take care of these debts before they become unmanageable.

Take a look at your spending habits. Having material goods now isn't important if you plan to become a successful investor. You will be able to buy that BMW or Mercedes you want later when you can really afford it. For now, your focus should be on being able to direct your financial resources into your investments so that you can grow your wealth over time. Expensive toys, like a new car, can be a large financial drain. If you have car loans, consider getting out of the car and into a used car that is reliable but costs a lot less. From this point forward, don't use debt to finance purchases. Keep a credit card on hand for emergencies, but don't use it to buy things like books or groceries that should be paid for using cash. If you can't pay for something with cash, it can wait.

Having an Emergency Fund

Life is never fair, and we are all going to encounter emergencies.

Recent studies have shown that most Americans don't have enough cash on hand to pay a $500 bill. If you are in that situation, you need to rectify it before you jump in with a large-scale investment plan. Remember that paying off debt first is always the priority. Debt is a sink that sucks important financial resources down the drain that could be used for other purposes. However, it's important to start putting money away for an emergency fund to be prepared for the unexpected — and being able to pay for it without having to take on more debt. Or worse, getting into a situation where you can't get credit but still need to find money to pay emergency bills. Set aside a small amount of money that you can start depositing into a savings account that you won't touch unless there is an emergency. Over time, the goal should be to have enough cash on hand to take care of emergency bills ranging up to $5,000 and to have funds on hand to cover times when you might be unemployed.

Consider Additional Sources of Income

If you have a large amount of debt or find yourself in a situation where coming up with a significant amount of money to invest is difficult, you should consider taking action to increase your income. There are many paths to consider. You can start by looking for a higher-paying job.

Alternatively, you can look into taking a second job, at least until you are in a better financial situation. Another approach that can be used is to either take on "gigs" or short-term contract work.

This can be done online or by doing some side work with companies like Uber. You can even look into starting your own online business to generate more income.

This doesn't have to be a permanent situation, but you are going to want to get to a place where you are debt-free and can put $1,000 or more into the stock market every month.

Net Worth and Changes Over Time

When you've gathered everything together, you'll want to determine your net worth. You are doing this for yourself, so don't be embarrassed if it's in a bad position right now. Simply add up the total current value of your assets and liabilities and subtract the total value of the liabilities from the total value of your assets. This is your net worth. If you can compare the value of each asset now to the value it had at the beginning of the year; you can also calculate the change in your net worth in percentage terms.

Are You Ready to Invest?

If you are debt-free or have a plan in place to take care of your debts and to build an emergency fund, you are ready to begin investing. The first rule of investing is to never invest more than you can afford to lose. If you go about your investment plan carefully, the chances of losing everything are slim to none. That said it's a wise approach to invest as if that could really happen. So, you shouldn't be investing next month's house payment or your kid's college funds in the hopes of gaining returns. After you have taken care of your debts and emergency fund, add up all of your basic living expenses, so you know how much you actually need per month. Anything left over above that is the amount of money you can invest for now.

Determining Your Financial Goals

Once you are in a position to invest something — even if you can only put in $100 a month now because you're paying off large debts — it's time to sit down and figure out your financial goals. There are several things to keep in mind:

Age: Generally speaking, the older you are, the more conservative you should be in your investment approach. The reason for this is simple. When things go badly, it takes time to recover and get back on the road to profitability. The older you are, the less time you have to grow your wealth in the future. That means a market crash, or a bad investment has larger consequences than it would have if you had thirty years to recover. Financial advisors generally recommend that older investors put their money in safer investments, which means putting some money into bonds and safe investments like US Treasuries that preserve capital. In the stock market, the older investor will seek out more stable companies that are larger, and while they may be growing, they have slow and steady growth with lower levels of risk. Of course, age can cut both ways. Many people reach their fifties with little to no savings or investment. If that describes your situation, you're going to want to invest more aggressively to seek rapid growth. Younger people also want to invest more aggressively, as they have a time horizon that permits taking on more risk. But time horizon isn't the only factor if you have no capital to protect; you definitely want to be more aggressive.

Chapter 3. Risks in Investing in Stocks

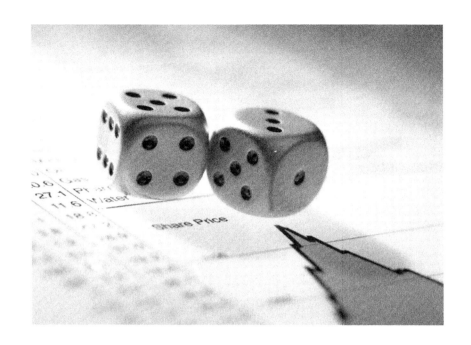

Understanding risk and volatility are two of the most important things to keep in mind with the stock market.

There are many different types of risk in the stock market. Some are direct, such as a small company that has the *potential* to make gains because of innovative products. Others are indirect and external. You can't manage all types of risks. Some come out of the blue, like the 9/11 terrorist attacks or the 2008 financial crash. So, if you think that you can control every form of risk, take a deep breath and realize you can't. In this chapter, we are going to try and describe every major category of risk investor's face, and if possible, we'll suggest ways to deal with them.

Emotional and Person Risk

First and foremost, you can control the risks to your investments that come from personal factors. These include fear, impatience, and greed. Emotions like these can be hard to control, but learning to take charge of them is essential if you are going to be a successful investor.

When real money is on the line, these emotions can become strong and overpowering. You must not let that happen.

The most common problem when it comes to emotions and personal risk is fear. When a stock market starts looking bearish, many investors immediately jump ship. They are making a huge mistake. A good investor is not getting in and out of the market at the slightest sign of a problem. In fact, selling off when everyone else is could be one of the biggest mistakes individual investors make. By the way, that doesn't exempt large investors. Many professional traders are subject to the same emotions and exhibit the same behavior during downturns. Massive selloffs are what cause bear markets to develop.

First of all, remember that you are looking to hold your investments over the long term. So, the ups and downs of the market and even recessions are not a reason to sell them. Over the past 50 years, by far the worst stock market contraction happened in the 2008 financial crisis. However, even that was short-lived. People that sold off their investments were either faced with being out of the markets altogether or having to get back in the markets when prices were appreciating. The lifetimes of other major bear markets were similar or even more short-lived. The first lesson in managing personal risk is to hold your investments through downturns.

The second lesson is that rather than giving into fear, you should start to see market downturns as opportunities. When prices are rapidly dropping due to a market sell-off, you should be buying shares. It's impossible to know where the bottom of a market is, and you shouldn't concern yourself with that.

At any time that share prices are declining, it's an opportunity, and so you should be making regular stock purchases. In one year, two years, or five years down the road, on average, the stocks that you purchased in a downturn are going to be worth quite a bit more.

The second problem that arises as a part of personal risk is greed. Many people start seeing dollar signs when they begin investing. Having a get-rich-quick mentality is not compatible with successful investing. Your approach should be centered on slowly and steadily accumulating wealth and not making a quick buck. As you invest, you're going to be coming across claims that certain trades or stocks are the next best thing, but you're better off ignoring such claims. More often than not, they turn out to be false. The stock market is not a gambling casino, even though many people treat it that way. You can avoid succumbing to greed by maintaining a regular investment program and not being taken in by the temptation that you can profit from short-term swings or "penny stocks" that are going to supposedly take off.

Finally, there is the related problem of impatience. After the Great Depression, people developed a more reasonable and cautious approach to the stock market. They realized that you're not going to get rich in six months or a year. The idea of long-term investing became dominant.

Unfortunately, in recent years, this lesson seems to be getting lost. More people are behaving like traders rather than as investors. Far too many investors are being taken in by the seduction of being able to beat market returns. Instead of being impatient, you should realize that you're in it for the long haul. Rather than trying to make a few extra bucks now, you're seeking to build wealth.

Risk of Loss of Capital

Obviously, financial risk is something you face when investing. Theoretically, there is a chance that you will lose all the money you invest in the stock market. This can happen if you tie your fate to a small number of companies. Several well-known companies like Lumber Liquidators, Bear-Stearns, and GM have either had major problems or gone completely under. Investors may have lost large sums in the process. The way to deal with this is to avoid investing in a small number of companies. Later in the chapter, we will investigate diversification as an investment strategy.

You'll also want to pay attention to the types of companies you invest in. Putting all of your money into small-cap stocks, for example, is probably a bad idea. So is putting all of your money into emerging markets, or into one sector of the stock market. Again, the key message is diversification. It's the way to protect you from financial risk.

Market and Economic Risk

Some factors are beyond your control, and the economy inevitably cycles through slowdowns and downturns. The market will cycle along with the economy, and also experience crashes when the economy may be doing fine overall. This happened in 1987, for example.

While these factors are not under your control, how you react to them is under your control. As we discussed in the section on emotional risk, you should not panic when there is a downturn. Remain level-headed, and use downturns as a buying opportunity. They are always followed by a brighter day; your job is to have the patience to wait for it to arrive.

Interest Rate Risk

Changing interest rates can impact the markets. Although this is a book about stock market investing, you should have some awareness of how bond markets work. You should also be aware that investor money can flow back and forth between bond and stock markets depending on conditions.

One thing that bond markets offer is the safety of capital, especially when we are talking about U.S. government bonds. When interest rates are high, U.S. government bonds (and other types of bonds, including corporate and municipal bonds) become very attractive.

Interest rate changes have risks for bond investors, however. Bonds are traded on secondary markets. When interest rates rise, bond prices fall because older bonds that offer lower interest rates become less attractive. Conversely, when interest rates fall, older bonds that pay higher interest rates have more value than new bonds being issued that pay relatively low rates.

This doesn't directly affect a stock market investor, but if demand for bonds rises, that can mean less capital flowing into the stock market. Less demand means lower prices, so the market may see declines.

Also, as we'll see, you can invest in bonds through the stock market using exchange-traded funds. If you are using this method, you'll want to keep close tabs on interest rates. That means paying closer attention to the Federal Reserve and its quarterly announcements. You should be doing so even if you are not going to invest in bonds in any way.

Announcements on interest rate changes can have a large impact on stock prices. But as always, keep your eye on the long ball. If the markets react negatively to an increase in interest rates that can be an opportunity to buy undervalued stocks.

Political Risk and Government

Government and politics can create big risks in the stock market. International events can cause market crashes, and these days even a tweet from the President can cause markets to rise and fall. Lately, some politicians have also been discussing breaking up the big tech companies. Others are talking about investigating them. Such talk — and worse actions— can have a negative impact on the markets. Part of your job as an investor is to keep a close eye on the news. You're going to want to know what's happening so that you can adjust if necessary.

Inflation Risk

Inflation hasn't been high in decades. However, in the late 1970s inflation rates were routinely in the double digits. Hopefully, that isn't going to be something that happens anytime soon, because high inflation rates can eat your returns alive. If the stock market is appreciating at 7% per year, but inflation is 14%, you can see that it's like having debt but investing in stocks — it's a losing proposition. Right now, inflation risk is very low, but you'll want to have some awareness of it and always keep tabs on it. High inflation rates also tend to go hand-in-hand with high interest rates, since the Federal Reserve will raise rates to try and slow down inflation. That means that bonds might become more attractive when inflation gets out of control.

Taxes and Commissions

Finally, we have the risk imposed by taxes. Of course, we are all going to be hit with taxes no matter where our money comes from. However, you need to take into account the taxes that you are going to pay when it comes to any gains you realize on the stock market. Part of being a successful investor is having an understanding of how much your taxes are cutting into your profits. If you are investing for the long-term, it will be less of an issue. But keep in mind that taxes can really eat into short-term trades. Frequent, short-term traders also face risk from commissions and fees. If you execute a lot of trades, the commissions can add up. This is not an issue for long-term investors.

Risk vs. Return

One of the fundamental trade-offs that an investor will make is risk vs. return. Generally speaking, the higher the risk, the greater the *possibility* of good returns. In 1998, Amazon was a pretty high-risk investment. While it had potential, major bookstores like Borders and Barnes & Noble dominated the space. Amazon was on shaky ground at the time, and another company could have come in and competed successfully for online book sales. That never happened, and Amazon ended up dominating book sales and expanding widely across retail and into cloud computing. That risk has translated into massive returns. A

$10,000 investment in 1998 would be worth more than $1 million today.

But hindsight is 20/20. Today, there are similar opportunities all around us, but it's hard to know which ones will end up being successful over the long term. If you are an aggressive investor, part of your job will be estimating which companies are the best bets for the future.

These examples serve to illustrate why a diversified portfolio is essential.

Managing Risk

There are a few time-tested strategies that have been developed that help manage risk. They even minimize, as much as possible, the kinds of risk that you will face that are completely out of control. That could include anything from a terrorist attack to interest rate changes.

These strategies are simple and easy to understand. The problem is that in practice, many investors fail to follow them, and instead let their decision-making be guided by emotions. You might end up following that path as well.

However, we are going to give you the tools you need to avoid it. It's up to you whether you utilize them or not.

Chapter 4. How to Invest in Stocks

(How to Buy Your First Stock)

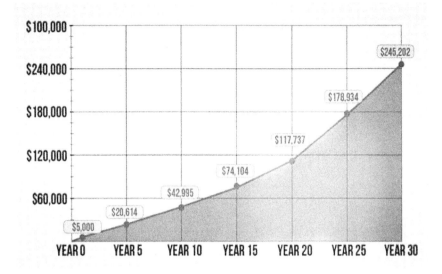

How to Get Start

Stock may seem incredibly intimidating for those starting in the investment world. It looks like a completely different world, and the hardest step for most is the beginning. However, it is quite simple to get started in stock investments. First, one must set goals for themselves and determine how they would like to invest in a stock. By writing down goals and ensuring that the investor's money is used in the best possible way, the investor is helping them yield the highest return on their investment. Once the individual's goals are made clear, they must plan on how to meet those goals. After this, they may choose the best investment method for achieving these goals. Then, it must be decided on where exactly the investor will go to invest their money. It is crucial, as this will be the platform by which the investor will trade their stocks. After this, the investor must open an account with whomever they choose. Before they start trading, the investor must make an initial investment using this account. While doing so, they may have to link their bank account to their stock trading account. The investor must then begin the process of buying and selling stocks using this account. Although this seems like a lengthy process, it is quite simple.

Planning and Meeting Goals

Investors must familiarize themselves with their goals. It is quite helpful to write down one's goals in each area and put them somewhere that is easily accessible. It is useful to have measurable goals to reach. This way, there may be a specific period and amount that may be assigned to the targets. It may help to come up with monthly goals. For instance, the investor may start with the purchase of 100 shares of stock in February. They may wish to increase that to 150 shares by March, 200 shares by April, and so on. This way, the investor may have a period to achieve their goals. It will allow them to measure their progress easily.

To set proper goals, one must reflect upon their past. How much will the investor be able to set aside for stock realistically? If one's goals are not realistic, it may become discouraging and set the investor back from their full potential. The investor must consider any past investments they have made. They must consider what worked and what did not. It is crucial to consider income and expenses when investing, and one must also consider any savings goals that one has. This will make it more apparent what may be invested in stocks.

Without a clear guide on how to invest, the investor will lack direction. It may lead to spur-of-the-moment decisions, and the investor may regret these choices. There may be some periods where one will not trade, as it won't be as profitable. Perhaps the market is down, and the trader does not wish to sell any stock. Perhaps the market is up, and the trader does not want to buy any stock. There will be events such as vacations, holidays, stressful events, or emergencies.

One must also consider how much money they have. Although it is possible to double one's money in a year, it is not likely for a beginner to do so. One may also choose to invest one time and hold it, or they may choose to invest more into their account often. This time and amount will depend on the investor and their financial situation.

The investor must also choose a strategy. They may wish to buy and sell stocks or to buy and hold stocks. They may even consider options trading. Whichever method that the investor chooses, there will be different goals to fit those strategies.

Long-term goals may be set to help the investor. Although planning for the following year may help the investor, longer periods may prove even more beneficial. Perhaps the investor wishes to acquire a million dollars worth of stock in the succeeding ten years. Perhaps the investor wishes to save a certain amount for retirement, which they wish to have by the next 25 years. Whatever the end goal is, the investor must make that clear so that they can begin working towards it immediately. Once a proper plan is created for meeting the investor's goals, they may move to the next step.

Choosing an Investment Method

After the investor has set goals and created a plan to meet them, it is time to decide on which investment method they wish to pursue. For those that wish to trade on their own completely, the DIY (do-it-yourself) method is the best fit. The investor may conduct all their trades online, making transfers from the bank manually or automatically. It will allow full control of one's investments. There will also be complete independence over what the investor wishes to buy and sell, how much they wish to trade, and how often they wish to trade.

They will, however, need to dedicate time to researching, making any transfers, trading, and other procedures. There is also a higher risk for this choice, as a beginning investor will not have the education that a financial advisor will. They also won't be under the control of a Robo-Advisor. However, all the profit that is made by the investor will be theirs to keep. They won't have to pay commission and fees outside of any required by the broker that they use.

The least independent approach to investing in stock is by hiring a financial advisor. It is for those who do not wish to touch their stock at all and to have it fully regulated for them. Hesitant beginners may benefit from this method. It is important to remember, however, that this method tends to be the costliest. It is most beneficial for those with higher assets and larger portfolios. It is also important to choose an investor that will work to meet the investor's goals, not just the goals of themselves. Therefore, the investor must set specific goals for themselves and how they wish to invest their money. They may more easily communicate with the advisor their desires, which may be carried out for them.

Choosing a Stockbroker

When investing for oneself, a proper stockbroker must be chosen. This will depend on the individual's needs and wants. For some, their bank that they already operate offers stock investments through their bank. This is a quick and simple option, as their money will already be linked through the bank, and they may already be familiar with their style. There may also be options for financial advisors in the bank that are free of charge. Otherwise, the investor must research their options before settling on a broker.

When choosing a stockbroker, the investor should research any fees (transaction fees, maintenance fees, etc.), minimum funds required to open an account, any commission collected by the stockbroker, and accessibility. The investor may prefer a specific type of formatting for their broker to have. There may also be free education, customer service, and other ways to make investing easier for the investor.

The investor must choose the option that will allow them to make the highest return on their investments. The investor should keep in mind which services they are likely to use most frequently, and they should choose the broker that charges the least to use those services. There may be transactional fees, which are costs for buying and selling stocks. Many beginning investors tend to forget this, so it is essential to take this into account.

Opening an Account

When opening an account, there are often a few steps that are required. This is typically not a lengthy process, but the investor should be aware of the potential actions associated with opening an account.

The first step when opening an online account is typically to create an account. This will consist of a username and password, as well as some personal information. This may include setting goals, determining which types of features the investor wishes to use, and the investor's experience level. This information will help to create the optimal experience for the investor.

There may also be an application for the account to ensure that the investor is qualified to hold the account. There may also be an agreement stating that the investor assumes all the risks of investing and understands that the money is not insured or guaranteed. Initial Investment and Linking Accounts

During the application process, the investor will most likely be prompted to fund the account. This can be done in several ways. The investor may transfer the funds electronically via an EFT (Electronic funds transfer). This is transferring the money from a linked bank account and will most likely only take one business day to transfer. The investor may also choose to make a wire transfer, which is a transfer directly from the bank. It is important to consider how much to invest in the account initially carefully. For those just starting, there may not be much money to invest at first. The minimum investment amounts for the broker should be looked over beforehand.

Buying and Selling Stocks

After the investor funds their account, it is time to start trading the stocks. It must be decided what stock, how much of the stock, and how the investor wishes to buy. Once these factors are decided, the investor must buy the stock. It is usually as simple as searching the stock symbol and selecting "buy." It is best to wait until the stock is at a low, but the investor must also begin investing as early as possible in experiencing the benefits of investing. When the stock is bought, it will typically take a bit to process and for the broker to receive these funds. After that, it will show up in the online portfolio of the investor. When it is time to sell this stock, the investor may typically visit their portfolio and click "sell" on the desired stock.

Chapter 5. When to Buy and Sell Stock

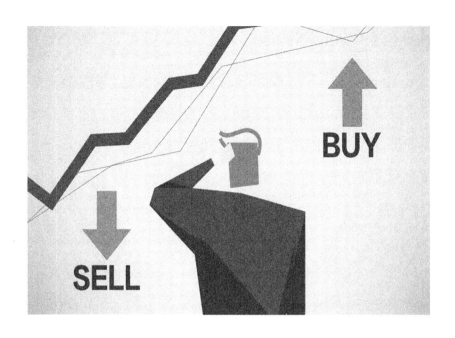

When to Sell a Stock

Determining when to sell a stock is a decision that even the world's best investors wrestle with. Warren Buffett has said that his holding period for a stock is forever. Does Buffett really hold every stock that he buys forever? Of course not! The point that he is making is that you should always purchase a stock with the intention of holding it forever; therefore, make sure your money has been put into your best investment ideas. An investor should leave his or her portfolio intact for at least five years, as long as the fundamentals for which a particular stock was purchased do not deteriorate. Investors should pay no attention to a stock's price volatility because it is a normal part of the investment cycle. As a long-term investor, there will be times when it makes sense to sell or reduce your position in stock earlier than you had planned. Next, we will talk about different circumstances in which you should consider selling a stock or reducing your position in a stock.

- **The Time Frame** — If you need the money within five years, it should not be invested in stocks. It would be best to invest your money in safe and stable short-term instruments. Money market accounts, money market funds, and short-term certificates of deposits would be better options. Since the Great Recession struck, some investment professionals now recommend that you not invest any money in stocks that will be needed within 10 years.

- **An Overvalued Stock** — When a stock is significantly overvalued, sell it. Take the proceeds from the sale and invest them into other undervalued stocks that you have researched. The P/E ratio is still one of the best indicators of value. For example, if a stock has traded at an average P/E of 15 for the last seven to 10 years and the business is thriving, but the stock currently trades at a P/E of 30 or more on consistent or increasing EPS, you should seriously consider selling the stock. The PEG ratio is also a very effective method for determining if a stock is now overvalued.

- **Too Much Debt** — Too much debt is dangerous for any business because there's always the chance that a business may be unable to pay its debt. Too much debt also puts a business at greater risk of failure if a downturn in the industry or economy were to occur. Upon entering the 2007 recession, thousands of businesses here in the United States literally disappeared overnight and that was before things really got bad.

- **Too Much Risk** — You have already learned the importance of staying away from investments that are too risky. Sometimes new management will come to a business and begin to implement new policies; along with that implementation, they will knowingly or unknowingly expose a business to greater risk. If you purchased the stock of a business that stayed away from very risky practices, but the business has now begun to display risky behaviors that make you uncomfortable, sell the stock and find yourself a better investment.

- **Loss of Competitive Advantage** — You have also learned that we should only be purchasing the stocks of businesses that have a durable competitive advantage. When a business changes its business model, resulting in it losing its competitive advantage, sell the stock.

- **The Portfolio Lacks Balance or Diversification** — It's very easy for your best performing stock to become the largest holding in your portfolio, and there's absolutely nothing wrong with that. The problem arises when the stock makes up more than 20-25% of your portfolio's total value. Legendary investor, Jim Slater suggests that individual investors limit the number of funds invested in a single stock within their portfolios to a maximum of 15%. When your portfolio becomes heavily weighted in one stock, consider reducing your position of that stock to bring more balance and better diversification into your portfolio.

- **Stock Reaches Its Fair Value** — Our goal as investors should always be to purchase a stock at a discount to its fair value and it is recommended at least a 25% discount to its fair value. By doing so, when you sell a stock that has reached its fair value, you are guaranteed a gain of at least 25% from the sale. This is a disciplined approach to selling a stock. According to research, it was common for Benjamin Graham to sell a stock once it had a 50% gain in price. If the future prospects of a particular stock look good, you may decide to sell only a portion of the stock, such as half of its shares, and hold on to the rest when using this approach.

- **When Your Analysis is Found to Be Flawed**— There will be times when an investor will be very detailed and careful in his or her analysis of a particular company or its stock, only to find out later that his or her analysis is incorrect or flawed. Whether a stock should be sold at that time depends on the seriousness of the error and its impact on the long-term performance of the business. So, when you find that you have incorrectly analyzed a particular business, it is essential for you to take a serious look at all available information to determine whether or not to sell the stock or to continue holding it. One thing is certain, as an investor, you will not always be right when analyzing a company or its stock.

There is no clear-cut way to determine the optimal time to sell a stock. There will be times that you will sell a stock because it has not performed well, only to see it skyrocket and double or triple in price soon after you sell it. There will also be occasions when you have purchased what seems to be the perfect stock, only to watch it tumble in price and for no apparent reason. Learn what you can from these events and move on. Even Peter Lynch, Jim Slater, and other great investors have sold stocks too early or too late. It's going to happen sometimes.

When to Buy a Stock

After the investor funds their account, it is time to start trading the stocks. It must be decided what stock, how much of the stock, and how the investor wishes to buy. Once these factors are decided, the investor must buy the stock. It is usually as simple as searching the stock symbol and selecting "buy." It is best to wait until the stock is at a low, but the investor must also begin investing as early as possible in experiencing the benefits of investing. When the stock is bought, it will typically take a bit to process and for the broker to receive these funds. After that, it will show up in the online portfolio of the investor. When it is time to sell this stock, the investor may typically visit their portfolio and click "sell" on the desired stock.

Starting out as a stock investor is quite simple. The investor must follow a few steps to become a stock trader. They must choose an investment method, select a stockbroker, open an account, a fund that account, and they will be ready to go.

Your very first stock trade can be frightening - not to mention confounding. You've done your stock research, you believe you've found a winner, and now you're all set to put your brand-new brokerage account to excellent usage and begin trading — nevertheless, you're not quite sure how to "carry it out."

Trade "execution" is just an elegant technique for describing an exchange. To "trade" typically describes a particular kind of investing method, so certifying your use of the term "trade" with "carry out" lets other financiers understand that you're going over a particular exchange.

The real-time it takes to perform your trade can move from broker to broker and market to market. (The SEC requires that all brokerage companies supply documents quarterly to the basic population about the handling of their customer orders).

Your broker will unquestionably put your order through their complicated trading computer system network to get a hold of your shares when you do put in your order. In many cases, your order will never ever leave the broker — your brokerage company ought to clean out shares of the organization you're purchasing from its stock.

You have a couple of choices when it comes to trading stocks beyond merely selling and purchasing. Basically, you get shares of a particular stock and sell them, relying on that the stock will diminish in worth, leaving the distinction between the selling rate and ultimate repurchase rate in your pocket.

Stock Order Types

Naturally, buying stocks is similarly more complex than only one purchase. There are numerous different approaches for considering your purchase, all going concerning cost, the time point of confinement, which is simply the start.

Anyhow, what are your alternatives for purchasing stock? There are 5 various types of stock orders that your broker will likely let you utilize.

A market order is a demand to sell a stock or buy at the existing market value. Market orders are quite a great deal for the basic stock order, and because the capability is typically performed instantly.

Something to keep as a primary top priority with a market order is the way you do not manage the amount you pay for your stock purchase or sale; the marketplace does.

The speed with which online market orders have actually launched might have made this less of a danger than it used to be. The market still moves quicker.

Some individuals do not have problems with this, for those that do this, imperfection can be met with a breaking point order.

- **Point of Confinement Order**

  A breaking point order can keep you from purchasing or selling your stock at a rate that you do not want, possibly assisting you in keeping a strategic range from a horrible choice. On the off possibility that the cost is a misdirected base and not in tune with the market, nevertheless, the order will never ever be made.

  Keep in mind that some brokers charge more for point of confinement orders, as the trade might not go through.

- **Stop-loss Order**

  Stop-loss orders, when that price is reached, transform into market orders. The target price is hit, and the trade is executed at market value.

- **Stop-Limit Order**

  Stop-limit orders are also stopped orders based on hanging tight at a particular expense. Stop-limit orders end up being point of confinement orders when the target cost is reached as opposed to market orders.

  Changing into a breaking point order can be something useful for a stop order, staying away from particular threats. On the occasion that the shares topple to $20.00 at the very same time, then instantly shoot back up, your market order might go through in any case.

- **Tracking Stop**

  Generally, this is a stop order based upon a portion modification in the market cost instead of setting a target cost.

  You can pick to what degree the order stays open when you put an order into your broker. Naturally, orders are day orders, indicating that they are signed up until completion of the trading day. Outstanding till-canceled orders stay open until you really enter and cancel them.

Chapter 6. How to Generate Passive Income from the Stock Market

Income investing is a little bit of a different ballgame than growth investing. In this case, we are seeking out companies that pay dividends. That means ignoring a lot of high growth stocks like Amazon and Netflix. It also means ignoring disruptive companies with potential like Tesla. When you are an income investor, you are looking to make a certain level of income from your stock holdings. That may be now, or it may be in the future. But your portfolio is going to look quite different from a growth investor, and even a value-oriented growth investor.

Yield

Start compiling a diverse list of companies that pay dividends that you find interesting. In each case, track the yield, which is the dividend divided by the share price. That will help you compare apples-to-apples when judging one dividend stock against another. Keep in mind that you are going to be seeking some kind of balance, so buying up stocks with the highest yields isn't the best philosophy. To see why to consider a company called consolidated communications. They pay a yield of 32%. The problem is, it's a penny stock. That means it's only $4 or so a share.

Most analysts are rating it a SELL. A glance at the chart indicates it has dropped from a $29 share price over the past couple of years, and yet it's still rated as being overvalued. These are major red flags.

Dividend

You may also be interested in the actual dividend payment, and not just the yield. IBM pays $6 a share, but Apple only pays $1.55 a share. So, you'd have to own more than three Apple shares for every share of IBM you could buy in order to get the same annual income from your stocks. Since IBM is cheaper on a per-share basis, that is something to take into consideration.

Dividend Growth

For any stock that you invest in, you're going to want to look at the history of their dividend payments. The ideal dividend stock is one that pays higher dividends over time. IBM is a great example because they paid consistent dividends through the 2008 financial crisis, and they have been increasing their dividends since then. Dividend growth ensures that your dividend payments will keep up with or exceed inflation.

DRIPS and Reinvesting

If you have a large amount of capital available right now, you can buy up shares of stock and start living off the dividend payments. However, if you are looking at a long-term investment program, you are going to want to reinvest your dividends. In the future, you're going to want to have as many shares as possible, so taking cash out now simply doesn't make sense. Instead, the payments from dividends should be used to purchase additional shares. Some companies even allow you to purchase fractional shares with the money.

A DRIP is a Dividend Reinvestment Program. In this case, the company will automatically take any dividends you earn and use them to buy additional shares. This will help enforce discipline in case you get tempted to cash out your dividends and waste the money on a trip or new car. Instead, the company will force you to save for the future.

Exchange-Traded Funds

The possibility of using exchange-traded funds to meet your investment goals always exists. In this case, you can seek out an ETF that invests in dividend stocks. You will still receive dividend payments, and the fund will have built-in diversification. When looking at ETFs to use for dividend investing, be sure to focus on yield, and pick funds that have the highest yields. Many investors can do a mixture of both; you could invest in ETFs while also investing in specific companies like IBM.

Alternative Investments

The world of dividend investing isn't restricted to traditional stock investing. You can also invest in the following:

- REITS

- MLPs

- BDCs

A REIT is a real estate trust. This is a company that owns hard property assets and rents them out. The types of property are quite varied. For example, you can invest in

REITs that own rental homes, apartments, or commercial real estate. There are also REITs that own hotels and resorts. In fact, any type of property that you can think of is represented by at least one REIT. But interestingly, there are REITs that have great prospects for the future because they are technology-related. For example, some REITs own cell phone towers, and there are others that own cloud computing.

REITs pay high dividends, and they trade like stocks on the stock market. Investing in REITs is a good way to get some exposure to real estate and other types of property ownership.

An MLP is a master limited partnership. These companies are midstream energy companies that transport oil and gas, own pipelines, or own refinement facilities. These are great investments to consider, and they also pay high dividends. You also invest in them by purchasing shares on the stock market. These types of investments are particularly noteworthy because the companies are partnerships and not corporations. When you invest, you become a limited partner. This means that you can deduct company expenses on your tax returns. Essentially, a large share of the income from an MLP is tax-free.

The final alternative investment that we are looking at is called a BDC, or Business Development Corporation. They also trade on stock exchanges and pay dividends. These are financial companies that invest in small to mid-sized companies that need cash. They can provide loans to companies or take an ownership stake.

When to Cash Out

Cashing out is a personal decision. By cashing out, in this case, we don't mean selling off your shares. What we mean is when should you stop reinvesting and start taking dividends as cash income. The answer is you start doing this when the level of dividend payments you receive starts matching your desired income.

Don't be afraid to shake up your portfolio. If you find an investment that suits your needs better than stocks you are currently invested in, then you should be ready to sell some of your shares and invest in the other stock. There is no reason for you to be locked into a particular stock, you can buy shares in other companies and then start getting dividend payments from them in the next upcoming cycle.

Fundamentals Always Matter

No matter which path you choose, when dividend investing, you want to pay close attention to the fundamentals. In the end, fundamentals are what matters. A company with good fundamentals is going to be a good investment. So, you'll want some trade-off between solid fundamentals, yield, and dividend payment that suits your goals. Remember to always think long-term.

Bond Investing

Finally, if you are looking for an income investing portfolio, consider buying exchange-traded funds that invest in bonds.

As we discussed earlier, there is a wide array of choices, allowing you to find the right amount of risk and the right interest payments. You'll want to look at the yields of the bond funds. Some have high rates of growth and high yields. That is, you can achieve growth as well as income by investing in bond funds too. The advantage of using ETFs is that you can avoid the hassle of trying to invest in bond markets.

Chapter 7. The Main Mistakes of a Beginner

Mistakes happen in every field, sector, and industry. Some are always anticipated, while others happened unexpectedly. When it comes to stock trading, there are several mistakes that you can make. Understanding these mistakes can help you avoid them, thus ending up successful in your stock investments. Here are some of the common mistakes made by most investors, beginners, and professional traders alike:

Failure to Understand the Trade

It is always wrong to invest in a trade or business you know nothing about. It is a great mistake to engage in stock trading when you do not understand the business and financial models involved. You can avoid this mistake by taking the time to research the stock market and stock trading before investing your money. Know the different markets, the driving forces, as well as trading procedures.

Most investors tend to buy stocks from the latest companies and industries they know very little about. Although such companies may look promising, it is difficult to determine whether they will continue to exist.

Understanding a specific company gives you a better hand over other investors. You will be able to make accurate predictions about the company or industry, which may bring you more profit. You will quickly tell when the business is booming, stagnating, or closing way before other investors get this information.

Individuals who do not take time to study companies miss out on future trends of these companies. Failing to establish such trends leads to several missed opportunities. For instance, a person who invests in a company that is higher than his capital may quickly lose all his investment. That is why it is always advisable that you invest in the industry you understand better. For instance, if you are a surgeon, you can invest in stocks that deal with medicine or related stocks. Lawyers can invest in companies that generate income through litigation, and so on.

Impatience

The stock market is for patient investors. It is a slow but steady form of investment. Although it bears various opportunities that can bring you money, you cannot make enough profit in one day. Most stock investors are always faced with the challenge of being patient. Some end up losing trade positions before they mature in the quest to make quick money. Exiting the market too early will always cost you some returns. As a new investor, you must never expect your investment portfolio to perform more than its capability, as this will always lead to a disaster. Remain realistic in terms of the time, duration, and resources needed to earn from the market.

Failure to Diversify

Another mistake that easily causes disaster is the failure to diversify. Professional investors do not have a problem with this since they can easily profit from a single type of stock. However, young investors must be able to diversify to secure their investment. Some of them do not stick to this principle. Most of these lose a great fortune as soon as they get onto the stock market. As you seek to invest, remember the rule of thumb governing stock diversity. This states that you should not invest more than 10% of your capital in one type of stock.

Getting Too Connected with a Certain Company

The essence of trading in stock is to make a profit. Sometimes, investors get too deep into a certain company that they forget that it is all about the shares and not the company itself. Being too attached to a company may cloud your judgment when it comes to stock trading since you may end up buying stocks from this company instead of getting the best deal on the market. As you learn more about companies, always remember that you are into the business to make money, besides creating relationships.

Investment Turnover

Investment turnover refers to the act of entering and exiting positions at will. This is one other mistake that destroys great investments. It is only beneficial to institutions that seek to benefit from low commission rates. Most stock trading positions charge transaction fees. The more frequently you buy and sell, the more you pay in terms of transaction fees. You, therefore, need to be careful when entering positions. Do not get in or exit too early. Have a rough idea of when you want to close positions so that you do not miss some of the long-term benefits of these positions.

Timing the Market

Market timing results in high investment turnover. It is not easy to successfully time the market. On average, only 94% of stock trading returns are acquired without the use of market timing. Most traders time the market as a way of attempting to recover their losses. They want to get even by making some profit to counter a loss. This is always known as a cognitive error in behavioral finance. Trying to get even on the stock market will always result in double losses.

Trading with Emotions

Allowing your emotions to rule is one of the things that kill your stock investment returns. Most people get into the market for fear of losses or thirst to make returns too fast. As a young trader, you must ensure that greed and fear do not overwhelm your decision-making. Stock prices may fluctuate a lot in the short-term; however, this may not be the case in the long term, especially for large-cap stocks.

This means that you may get lower profits in the short term, but these may increase in the long term. Understanding this will help you avoid closing trades when it is not the right time yet.

Setting Unrealistic Expectations

This always occurs when dealing with small-cap stocks such as penny stocks. Most investors buy such stocks with the expectation that the prices will change drastically. Sometimes this works, but it is not a guarantee. To make great fortunes, people invest a lot of capital in these stocks, and then the prices do not change much. If these investors are not prepared for such an eventuality, they may feel frustrated and may quit the business completely. However, this is something that you must be able to manage if you want to grow your investment. Do not expect more than what a certain type of stock can deliver.

Using Borrowed Money

This is probably one of the greatest mistakes that investors make. Some investors get carried away with the returns they are making. As a way of getting more profits, they borrow money and use it to enter more stock positions. This is a very dangerous move and can result in a lot of stress. Stock trading is like gambling. You are not always sure how much you take home at the end of each trade. It is therefore not advisable for you to invest borrowed money in it.

As you try to avoid these mistakes, you must also avoid getting information from the wrong sources. Some traders have lost a fortune because they relied on the wrong sources for stock information. It is important to isolate a small number of people and places where you will seek guidance from. Do not be a person that follows the crowd. Take time before investing in new stock opportunities. Carry out proper due diligence, especially with small-cap stocks since these involve a lot of risks. Remember, you must trade carefully and implement expert advice if you want to succeed in stock trading.

CRASH COURSE

Chapter 8. Insider Tricks Used by Professional Traders

An investor should always be on the lookout for signals that might be clues about their investments. One signal you should be keeping an eye on is the actions taken by the insiders with a company. Are they sticking by the company and investing in it? Or do they seem to be running away from it despite amazing stock prices? These can be important clues as to the health and intermediate future of the company. One thing you need to keep tabs on is whether or not the insiders are buying or selling shares of the company. You'll also want to note major departures from the company. Of course, the company is going to make up some pleasant story about why some major figure is leaving. You know, they want to spend more time with their grandmother. But is that really what's going on? If other news or more signals are indicating otherwise, including insider moves, you might view such news with a negative eye. People often leave a sinking ship.

Insider Trading

Here we aren't talking about criminal activity, but rather a company members themselves who own shares of the company that they are associated with. A good indication that people are confident in the future of their company is finding out that they own and are buying more shares of stock in their own company. On the other hand, if they are selling off their shares, that can be a sign that the people actually running the company or involved with it don't have that much confidence in its future.

It's actually possible to find out what company insiders are doing when it comes to shares of stock in their own company. The Securities and Exchange Commission requires them to file publicly available reports. You can find publicly filed reports on a government website known as "Edgar." It can be found here:

https://www.sec.gov/edgar.shtml

"Insiders" will file various forms, including an initial form that they have to submit to the government indicating their insider status with the company. This is called form 3.

If you are researching this data, you're going to want to pay special attention to form 4 and form 144. On form 4, any transactions involving a large number of shares are recorded. So, if the insider bought a large number of shares, it would be recorded on form 4. Also, if they sold a large number of shares, it's going to be reported on form 4.

If a single insider is selling shares, that doesn't necessarily mean anything. However, if you notice that multiple insiders are off-loading their shares, pay attention. That might be an indication that a large number of people who are in the know about the company's prospects aren't confident about the company's future.

Form 144 is related to a special class of stock called restricted stock. This is stock that the insider was provided as compensation for employment. If they decide to unload it after a required holding period, this will be noted with form 144.

In summary, if insiders are confident that the company is doing well and has solid long-term prospects, they are probably going to be buying shares in the company, not trying to get rid of them. You will want to take this kind of information and incorporate it into the larger picture of course. It's important to consider all the indicators for the company and not get lost in the details of focusing on one sign. So, if you notice that there is a large sell-off, you'll want to check other information like the company's latest earnings reports.

Quantity also Matters

Don't get alarmed if people sell a small number of shares. When they are trying to divest their own portfolio of any interest in the company, it is when you should take notice.

Congressional Insiders

A few years ago, the news program 60 Minutes did an interesting investigation. They found that members of Congress were playing the role of insiders at many companies and getting advantageous stock buys as a result. Unfortunately, there isn't much we can do about that, but it's good to have awareness about it.

Stock Buybacks

Stock buybacks can be a good sign or a bad sign. If a company is doing well, a stock buyback can be used as a way for a company to pass on profits to investors. However, stock buybacks can also be an indicator that a company is heading for trouble. The first thing to consider is that the company has lower than expected earnings. In that case, a company might use a stock buyback in order to artificially boost their indicators on the stock market. Buying back shares of stock, if done on a large enough scale, can alter important metrics like the price per earnings ratio and earnings per share. If you have fewer shares but the same earnings, earnings per share are going to look more favorable. They can do this in the hopes of artificially boosting the value of the stock and hence it's the market price. Consider an example. Suppose that a company has $500 in earnings and 100 shares. The earnings per share are $5. If they buy back 50 shares, then you still have $500 in earnings, but with 50 shares, so now the earnings per share are $10. That looks better to investors taking a cursory look at the stock, but in reality, the company's prospects haven't changed.

Another negative possibility is that the company has stagnated. If companies are out of ideas and not pursuing new ones, they aren't investing a large amount of money into research and development. That means they have cash sitting around and using a stock buyback could be a simple way to unload the cash.

You'll also want to check the price-to-earnings ratio and look up to see if the stock is overvalued. It can be a bad sign when a company is buying back overvalued shares.

Another question to ask is, where is the company getting the cash used for the buyback? Hopefully, they have enough money on hand to do it. But if they are borrowing money for the share buyback, that is definitely a sign that the company is unhealthy.

If you have invested in a company and they engage in a share buyback, you'll want to investigate further to find out what's behind it. In many cases, it's not something to worry about. However, sometimes it's an indicator that the future with this company is not so bright.

Stock Splits

Another corporate action you will need to be aware of is a stock split. Companies can do stock splits or reverse stock splits. In a stock split, a share is converted from 1 share to 2 or 3 or more shares. That immediately changes the price per share and impacts metrics like earnings per share. Imagine that a company has a share trading at $100, and it has 100 shares outstanding, and earnings per share of $5, meaning they have a price to earnings ratio of $20. If they do a 2-1 split, now there are 200 shares. The amount of money invested in the company hasn't changed, so the share price immediately drops to $50 a share. Now you have twice the number of shares in your portfolio, so the value of your investment hasn't changed. Earnings per share would be cut in half and would be reported as $2.50. The price-to-earnings ratio would remain at $20.

One reason a company might do a stock split is to reduce the price of a share, in order to attract more investors.

A stock trading at $1,000 a share might be unaffordable for a lot of small investors. If a company was interested in attracting more small investors, they might to a 4-1 stock split and drop the share price to $250 per share. A stock split for a high-priced stock can also increase liquidity. That is, it will increase the ease with which you can sell your shares. Very high-priced stocks will have large bid-ask spreads, which can make them harder to sell. Doing a split and bringing the price back down to a lower level can reduce the bid-ask spread and make it easier for investors to sell their shares.

A reverse stock split is going to reduce the number of shares that you own. So, if you own 100 shares and they did a 1-2 reverse split, you would only own 50 shares after that. If the share price had been $100, it would rise to $200 after the split. Remember that the amount of money invested remains the same before and after the split, so the share price also has to change if the number of shares changes.

Chapter 9. Tips and Tricks for Successful Stocks Trading

There are some tips and tricks that you can keep up your sleeve to help you invest in stocks. Let us look at some of them.

Always Be Informed

You need to be informed about what happens in the market. This is the only way you can trust your decisions. You should go through different resources and publications if you want to obtain more information about the various stocks in the market.

Buy Low, Sell High

This is a strategy that most investors will use. It is always good to buy low and sell high, and you must follow this to the tee. It is when you do this that you can expect to make large profits in the market. When you buy low and sell high, you will purchase a stock at its lowest value and sell it at its highest value. It will be easy for you to determine when the stock price will reach the highest rate based on some methods and data you collect. You need to ensure that you always act according to the data that you have collected. Experts recommend that it is a good idea to buy stocks the minute the market opens. Most stocks reach their highest price in the afternoon, and that is when you should sell them.

Scalping

This is a very popular technique in the stock market. When you use this technique, you can always buy and sell stocks within a matter of a few seconds. Your purchases and sales depend on how fast you are. This is a very strange method, but it is very effective, especially in volatile markets. Let us assume that you purchased a stock at 10:00 A.M. and sold it at 10:02 A.M. The price of that stock is $3, and the selling price is $5. So, in a matter of two minutes, you made a $2 profit per share, and this is a great profit for a scalper. This does not seem like a profit, but if you do this at least twenty or thirty times a day, you can make a huge profit. You should only use this form of trading once you have enough experience in the market. If you want to take up this technique, you should have at least a year's worth of experience to help you make the right decisions.

Short Selling

Many traders use the concept of short selling when they invest in the market. Short selling refers to when you need to borrow stock from the holder and sell it to another buyer. Then, you will wait for the stock price to fall before you give the stocks back to the lender. This is one of the easiest ways in which you can capitalize on the volatility of the prices. You must make the right decisions about the investments you make and not invest or borrow useless stocks. You must always ensure that you maintain a wide margin that will make a few mistakes. You should ensure that you have enough capital to support any other investments if things never work out. It is always good to buy shares back at the earliest if you believe that the price of the stocks will continue to increase.

Identify the Pattern

It is important to remember that stocks and every other stock in the market will follow a pattern. Once you notice this pattern and understand it, you can invest in stocks successfully. This pattern has all the information you need about the high and low points of the stocks and gathers some information on how you can trade between those points. It is important to have the history of the stock with you since it will help you determine the previous trend and predict the future trend of the stock.

Look at the Results

Every company is result-oriented, which means that the report published by the company will tell you how well the company is doing. The report that the company shares will shed some light on how well it is doing in the market. You should go through this report to ensure that you are making the right choice. The data collection results should show you that you could make enough profits when you invest in it. A small company will always aim to sell a large volume of stocks, and if you are impressed with the company and its numbers, you can invest in the stocks of that company. Remember that a company only publishes the results quarterly. Therefore, you need to look at all the results before you invest in the company.

Look at the Company Name

When choosing to invest in the stock market, you should understand that its name does matter. You must see if the company is well known and is doing well in the market. You can invest in a company that does not have any significant changes. Some people steer clear of such companies. If you are not a fundamentalist and are willing to take on a few risks, you can use technical analysis to help you make the decision. It is always good to learn more about the company if you choose to invest in shares in that company.

Understand the Company Better

You need to look at how the stock performs in the market, but it is important to spend some time understanding the company you are investing in. You need to know if the company is working on the right products and services. Understand the industry of the company. See if they are developing new products, technology, or services. Remember that whatever the company does affects the price of the stock. The best way for you to do this is to learn more about the company through fundamental analysis.

You should always read the news about the company too. It is only this way that you can assess how well the company is doing. If you have any knowledge about the company or the products, you should spend some time to see where the company is heading.

When you start looking at a company, you need to ensure that you obtain the information from the right sources. Read this information carefully to understand whether the company is doing well or not. Ensure that the sources you use to obtain this information are reliable. If you get a fax, tip, or email from a person stating that one company is better than the rest, you need to make sure that you do not rush into investing. Take some time out and read about the company. Never invest in any company simply because of some information you may have received. Always conduct thorough research before you invest in the company. This is the only way you will learn if the company is doing well or not. Never waste your time or money. So, always stick to reliable sources and use that information to invest in the correct stocks.

Don't Trust Mails

You mustn't trust any emails that come from companies that claim to have enough knowledge about the stocks of other companies. These emails will also suggest the stocks that you should invest in, but the information in those emails is untrue. Companies cannot go through their investors' portfolios and suggest which stocks they should invest in. Even if a company does choose to do this, they may give you a suggestion that will not work for you. So, it is good to avoid these stocks and only invest in those stocks that you have all the information about.

Understand the Corrections

Remember that the price of stocks will be corrected in the market, and it is important that you remain patient. The price of the stock will drop when the market is correcting the price of the stocks in the market. If you are impatient, you will make a mistake and lose a lot of money. Always look at the company and make the right decisions about your investments. If a stock is either overpriced or underpriced, it means that the corrections will be made soon. Never sell your stocks in a panic and wait for the corrections to be made. You need to follow the news regularly, so you understand how or why the correction is being made.

Hire a Broker Only If Necessary

You should never hire a broker to do the job for you unless you need one. The only reason is that a broker will charge you a fee for helping you with your investments. They will also ask you to pay a commission, which will eat into your profits. You also need to remember that you need to pay your broker a fee regardless of whether you make a profit. So, they do not have to work hard to ensure that you make a profit. There are theories that companies hire brokers to increase the price of the stock in the market. They request the brokers to motivate investors to trade in a specific stock even if they do not want to invest in that stock. You will purchase these stocks if you can be swayed easily, which will lead to huge losses. You should always look for discounts online and see if you can trade independently. Avoid depending on your broker to buy and sell your stock.

Diversify Your Risks

This has been mentioned repeatedly across the book, so you can imagine how important it is for you to do this. You must always diversify your risks depending on the type of investment you make. This holds for any instrument. When you choose to invest in stocks, try to invest in stocks from different industries and sectors. If you invest in stocks only in one sector, you will lose a lot of money if the industry were to crash. It is because of this that you need to ensure that you diversify your capital. You must invest in different instruments in the market. Yes, one industry may be doing well compared to other industries, but this does not mean that you put all your money on stocks in that industry.

Money Movement

If you notice a sudden change in the price movement and the flow of money in the company, you know that the stock value will increase. If there is a sudden increase in the capital through external sources or it pumped its profits into its business, then it means that the company wants to expand. This will mean that the stock prices will rise, and it will benefit you as an investor. You must always keep track of the news and make the right decisions.

Look at the Stock Volume

If you notice that the volume of the stock has suddenly changed in the market, it is always a good idea to invest in that stock. The sudden changes in the price and volume of the stock will happen when there is some information in the news about the stock that makes people buy or sell stocks. Ensure that you capitalize on these situations so that you can make a huge profit. According to Timothy Sykes, you should always purchase a stock if you experience a high price after one year. The price of the stock will change only when the company talks about its earnings and bonuses.

Chapter 10.   Advice to Minimizing Losses and Maximizing Gains

Some firms have different shares on the market. Some are good, and others are not so lucrative. How are you going to pick the right companies' stocks to make a full profit?

Well, the question is a million dollars one, but the answer is pretty easy. Before and unless you know the stock market, the answer to the million-dollar question cannot be sought. Yeah, business awareness is a must for anyone who wants to invest in stocks.

The good news is that trading on the Internet is very easy and hassle-free. All can invest in the stock at any time. Unlike other investment options on the market, there is no lock-in duration and restrictions.

However, you have to do some simple work in this sort of investment. At first, you will certainly reap the rewards of your investment if you prepare correctly and acquire ample knowledge of the workings of the stock market.

When the initial groundwork has been done, the answer to the million-dollar question can be sought. If a corporation issued public stock on the market — you bought those stocks, for instance, 100 shares at $10 each. Now, what factors will affect the price of the share? First and foremost, we must know why a specific company issues the public shares — the main purpose of shares issuance is to raise money for business expansion or pay the debt if any, and with the business increasing, the share prices often increase accordingly.

On the other hand, if you buy a share of a company and the share price falls in a few days, the company's growth curve is decreasing. Expert professionals, therefore, often recommend that investors keep an eye on major shares in the company.

Even if you have no idea what a company is, you can access information about a company, its growth curve, and its credibility in the previous industry. Many professionals recommend that they even purchase small-scale shares for full benefit.

Whenever you plan to buy a company share — gather all of the company's profile details and other important information. Following the study, purchase certain shares if you agree that a certain company share price will increase.

What Other Factors Affect the Trading Process?

Well, the website of the stock trading organization, the stockbroker, and the decision-making capacity impact the entire trading mechanism directly. It is always often easier to make a thorough market analysis on the Internet and then select the best alternative. If your fundamentals are simple, your investment will certainly give you maximum benefit. It is easier to do some simple work and then trade instead of jumping straight on the market. Now it is clear that professionals who make money on the same market have done all the required work required before the trade. So if you are a new investor and want to earn profits in a short time, first do your primary job, advise financial experts and then start trading online. Save money and build a good financial reserve to help your family better and effectively.

Options Trading — Losing Before Winning

Many options traders were frustrated when they set options to make a profit faster. Currently, nearly 90 % of the time, your options role will lose a lot until it would ultimately gain if it's raining at all. Sounds like something you've experienced?

Yeah, this is a reality of options trading and practice that seasoned traders like me learned to embrace. Many of my positions, especially single directional ones such as a long call, actually fall into a 60% loss until they eventually return to an astounding 100% profit. Yeah, most beginners took the loss early and missed the benefit.

What is the explanation for this phenomenon?

There are three key reasons why MOST options strategies lose a lot before making a profit.

The bid/work distribution of all the options involved in one position is first and foremost. The difference between the demand price and bid price of the options contract is the bid differential. Traders purchase retail options at the requested price and sell at the sale price.

An Options Contract with a $0.90 demand price and a $0.60 offer price has a $0.30 bid transaction range. This means that if you sell the option right as you purchased it, you instantly lose $0.30. The range of requests for options is considerably large for most inventories with spreads of $0.30 and spreads of up to $0.50 in some cases.

Only in extremely liquid inventories such as the QQQQ are there spreads of $0.10. Buying out money options costing about $0.70 with a bid of $0.20 could make you lose up to 30% right when you're in a spot! This is where most beginner options traders freak out, particularly if they commit the greatest sin of options trading—put all of their money into one trading.

Secondly, none of us, either George Soros or Warren Buffett, are stock market wizards. None of us will be able to trade reliably and move the stock exactly as planned at the moment it was launched (day trading excluded because periods are very limited in day trading).

As Jim Kramer said, we should always gradually develop a role over days because we are not geniuses. Yeah, unfortunately, most of the time, the stock seems to be heading in the opposite direction the very moment you sell.

The explanation seems that most traders enter trade emotionally when the shopping is heavy, which is also the point at which the stock retreats somewhat because of the over-compensation or over-sale when purchasing put options or shortcuts.

Leveraging in options trading now works in both ways. If it makes money faster, it will lose money faster, even though the stock just marginally shifts towards your favor.

Thirdly, Feedback!

Yeah, for a certain number of contracts, most options brokers will charge a minimum of $10 per trade. For beginner traders who take very small jobs, $20 ($10 for purchases and $10 for sales) may make considerable losses, particularly when money options are purchased. Committees often greatly sacrifice nuanced techniques for alternatives with multiple legs, such as the Condor Spread.

Combine the offer for spread loss with a pullback into the market, because we're not geniuses, and you'll end up losing 60% or more the very day that you placed a stock option. Sad but true, such a drastic and rapid loss would ruin most policy losses.

That is why many traders take losses too early to see stock recovery, ultimately in the right direction. Yeah, most losses are taken before the expiry of certain options! From a recent report, 60% of all available options were shut down before expiry!

When we use options trading strategies with limited risk, we can restrict this risk to a sum that we fully expect a loss, and we can tolerate loss if the trade goes wrong. When we transact directional options, we place some small "bets" over some time, and each time, ensure that the total is small enough to lead to negligible losses if the trade goes badly.

When you traded in this way, strength and control will overpower your emotions in the face of almost an immediate 60% loss in directional options trading.

Holding control also enables non-geniuses like us to wait for the reserves where they would ideal are, as most inventories won't move the way we want them to instantly (neutral tactics for options are very different, as you would expect the inventory not to move.

If you embrace the fact that your next trade option will possibly lose money considerably before they can benefit, it means you can use only the money that you intend to lose from the beginning to have a holding power that increases your chance of winning considerably

Chapter 11.   Tax Implication and How to Reduce Their Impact on Your Earnings

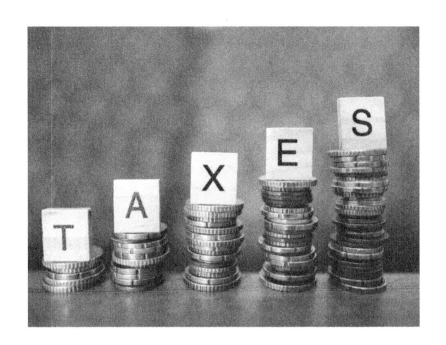

Ah, we come to our favorite subject, taxes! The objective in the stock market is to make money, and every time that you make money, you are going to find yourself in a position of having to pay taxes on it. Unfortunately, it's a reality we can't escape. You might delay it, but at some point, you're going to have to pay.

There are many different issues you need to be aware of when it comes to taxes. This isn't a tax advisory book, and you should consult an accountant to make sure you're doing everything right. However, we'll take a brief look at some of the main issues.

Capital Gains

Suppose that you hold an asset, and the price appreciates. If you sell it, you'll realize a capital gain — in other words, you made money. When you make money by selling appreciated assets, you owe capital gains tax. The important thing to consider is how long you held the asset.

If you held the asset for one year or less, this is a short-term capital gain. The bad news about this is short-term capital gains are considered ordinary income. That means you'll pay the regular income tax rate on your gain.

If you hold the asset for longer than a year, even if it's just a day, then it becomes a long-term capital gain.

For some reason, Congress has decided that they know that holding assets for an arbitrary period that they made up is better, and so long-term capital gains have very favorable tax rates. These are much lower than income tax rates.

The bottom line here is that you'll want to take into account how long you have held an asset (aka stocks) when selling. If you are a long-term investor and planning to hold your investments until retirement, this means that you will be paying long-term capital gains taxes on your investments when you sell them off to get the money. Of course, if your retirement is in the distant future (more than ten years away), it's hard to say what the laws are going to be.

Dividend Income

The important thing to note about dividend income when considering taxes is that it's considered to be ordinary

139

income. There isn't anything special to consider dividend income. The one exception is dividends paid by an MLP. That's because they aren't technically dividends and you're considered a "partner" in the business. In that case, you are able to deduct depreciation from your taxes. The company passes it on to the "partners." This has huge implications. Many investors in MLPs are able to enjoy their income from the investments virtually tax-free. It's a little complicated, so if you start putting money into MLPs, you'll want to consult an accountant. The company will be sending you the appropriate forms.

Individual Retirement Accounts

One of the advantages of individual retirement accounts or IRAs is that they allow investments to grow inside of them tax-free. You can utilize this to your advantage. One way to do so is to buy dividend stocks inside the IRA and then reinvest the dividends. That way, you can continually grow your account and grow it beyond the usual limitations.

Expenses

Deducting expenses related to your investment might be problematic. The IRS isn't too friendly when it comes to deducting expenses related to investing. There is one exception, and that is if you are a day trader. Then a day trader can deduct expenses like publications they read and all the computer equipment and software services that they sign up for. But if you are doing ordinary investing, that might be a hard sell.

One way to get around it is to set up a business to run your investing. Then have the business buy all the equipment and so forth. Of course, this will inject other complications into the situation, so you'll have to weigh the pros and cons in order to determine whether or not it's really worth the extra hassle. Quite frankly, in most cases, it's not going to be.

Understanding Your Brokerage Account and Statement

You'd be surprised to know that most extremely wealthy people have taxable brokerage accounts. It provides an avenue for them to benefit from the stock market and diversify their income stream. As we've discussed earlier in this book, if you want to invest huge amounts of money and be a successful investor, you have to open a taxable brokerage account.

What is a Brokerage Account?

A brokerage account is a taxable investment account that you can use to buy and sell stocks and other securities. As the name suggests, it's opened through a brokerage firm. It's much like a bank account. You have to deposit money into your account before you can start buying and selling stocks.

You can deposit money into your account through checks or electronic funds transfers. You can also wire money to your account.

Type of Investments a Brokerage Account Can Hold

Brokerage accounts are not just for stocks. There are a number of securities that a brokerage account can hold, including:

- **Common Stock** — This represents partial ownership of a company. It usually comes with voting rights.

- **Preferred stock** — This stock usually comes with high dividend payments, but it's more expensive than common stock. Preferred stock shareholders typically don't have any voting rights.

- **Bonds** — A bond is a debt security. When you purchase a bond, the issuer (usually a government entity) owes you money. You earn money from bonds through interest rates.

- **Mutual Fund** — A mutual fund is funded by different shareholders. It's basically a pool of money that's invested in different securities. It's relatively easy to invest in a mutual fund. Plus, it's usually managed by a financial professional. You can buy different mutual funds, too, so you don't have to put all your money into one mutual fund.

- **ETF** — An ETF, or Exchange Traded Fund, is a basket of different securities that are traded like a stock. An ETF is a good investment because it has trading flexibility. It helps you diversify your investment portfolio and manage risk. It's also cheaper than a traditional mutual fund.

- **REIT** — A real estate investment trust, or REIT, is a company that either finances or operates income-producing real estate properties, such as commercial buildings. REITs usually own various income-generating real estate companies, such as hospitals, warehouses, hotels, and malls. You can invest in publicly traded REITs using your brokerage account.

- **Money Market and Certificate of Deposit** — A money market account generally represents pools of liquid mutual funds. It has higher interest rates and has a limited check-writing capacity. A certificate of deposit is basically a time deposit. For example, you agree to deposit $10,000 into your account. You can't withdraw that amount for five years, but you'll earn an interest rate throughout this period. So, if you earn $1,000 in interest per year, you're going to earn an extra $5,000 for your deposit after five years.

Cash Brokerage Accounts and Margin Brokerage Accounts

There are two main brokerage account types — cash accounts and margin accounts. A cash brokerage account requires you to deposit cash into your account. You'll have to pay for your transactions in cash and in full when you have a cash brokerage account.

A margin account, on the other hand, allows you to borrow from the broker using some of your assets as collateral to buy securities.

If you're a beginner, it's best to go for a cash brokerage account. Why? Well, margin brokerage accounts are complex and will get you buried in debt if you're not careful.

Limits of Money You Can Deposit in a Brokerage Account

As previously mentioned, other investment plans such as the IRA and 401(k) have limits, but taxable brokerage accounts do not, so you can deposit and invest as much as you want. That said, keep in mind that you do have to pay taxes for this type of investment.

How Many Brokerage Accounts Can One Have?

You can have as many brokerage accounts as you want, but keep in mind that most brokerage firms require a minimum deposit amount of $500 to $2000, so opening multiple accounts can be costly.

However, if you have unlimited resources, you can open multiple accounts with different brokerage firms.

Difference between a Discount Broker and a Full-Service Broker

There are two general types of broker:

- A full-service broker and

- A discount broker

A full-service brokerage account is great because it comes with a dedicated broker. You can call, text, or email him should you want to make an order. This broker usually knows you personally, and sometimes he knows your family. He also knows your finances intimately. He's like a financial advisor. You usually have to meet him regularly to discuss your portfolio.

Full-service brokers usually charge high commission fees. A discount broker, on the other hand, doesn't charge much. But, this type of broker usually operates online. A discount brokerage account is like a Do It Yourself (DIY) investment plan.

So, what should you choose? Well, it depends on what your priority is. If you are on a budget and you really want to save money, it's best to open a discount brokerage account. But, if you really want to have a financial adviser, it's a great idea to open a full-service brokerage account.

Understanding Your Broker's Statement

A broker's statement is a monthly report that contains the activities in your brokerage account. You can choose to receive a paper statement, but you can usually just check it online as well.

It pays to examine your statement carefully so you can spot some kind of fraud. When you first receive your income statement, you have to check to see if it looks professional. An unprofessional-looking statement is a red flag. Legitimate brokerage firms invest time and effort to make sure that their reports look polished and professional.

Here's what you'll find in your broker statement:

- **Statement Period Date** — A broker's statement reports how your investment is doing at a specific period of time, usually a month. If you don't see a statement period date, that's a red flag.

- **Account Number, Account Name, and Address** — This obviously contains your taxable brokerage account number, your name, and your present address. Be worried if this information is incorrect.

- **Contact Information** — This contains the contact information of your broker. If you don't see this anywhere in the statement, the brokerage firm you're dealing with may be dubious.

- **Name of the Clearing Firm** — This contains the name and the contact number of the clearing firm that holds your investments. FINRA rules require brokerage firms to place this information in their statements. So, be alarmed if you don't see this anywhere in your statement.

- **Account Summary** — This provides insight with regards to how your account is doing. This can help you review and assess your investment decisions.

- **Fees** — This covers the transaction and commission fees you've paid within the time period.

- **Account Activity** — This is where you can see the stocks you've bought or sold within that particular time period.

- **Margin** — If you have a margin account, you'll find this section. This contains the amount you've borrowed to purchase stocks and other securities.

- **Portfolio Detail** — This section breaks down your investment by types like stocks, bonds, or mutual funds.

Chapter 12.   What to Do and

What to Buy in a Down Market

Now that you have an idea of why you need to invest and some fundamental principles in investment as well as asset classes, you can invest in it. For you to start winning in a big way, you would have to put in the time. You would have to put in the effort. You would have to have the proper experience and groundwork to make that happen. And in many cases, even with the best-laid plans and with the best strategies laid out, things still don't pan out.

The better approach is to do the best with the situation you are facing. In other words, use specific strategies that would enable you to position yourself to come out ahead. They might not necessarily result in you making tons of money or experiencing truly stupendous returns, but they can position you for solid gains. The following strategies enable you to do just that.

Buy Depressed Assets

Now, this might seem straightforward. After all, this is just a reiteration of the classic investment and commercial maxim of "buy low, sell high." However, the big challenge here is in determining what constitutes a "depressed asset."

You might be thinking that a stock that was trading at $50 and pops to $150 might not be all that depressed if it fell to $100. You might be thinking, where's the depression? This is not a fire sale. It hasn't fallen enough.

If you look at the stock's trajectory and how much growth potential and market attention, it might very well turn out that the stock is headed to $300. Do you see how this works?

If that's the case, then scooping up the stock at the price of $100 after it fell from $150 is a steal. After all, buying something worth $300 for a third of its price is one heck of a bargain.

Now, the big issue here is how do you know the stock's full future value? This is where serious analysis comes in. You can't just buy stocks on hype. It would be best if you looked at facts that would inform the growth trajectory of that stock.

For example, is it a market leader? Does it have certain drugs in the approval pipeline that have little to no competition? Is it on the cusp of a breakthrough drug patent? Is it in the process of buying out its competition?

There are many factors that you should consider, which can impact the overall future value of a stock. You should pay attention to its current developments, and you should pay attention to the news cycle surrounding the company.

You should also pay attention to its industry. Is its industry fast-expanding, or is it a "sunset industry" on its last legs? If it's in a sunset industry, there might still be opportunities there because, usually, such industries witness a tremendous amount of consolidation. Whatever the case may be, always be on the lookout for the future value of a stock based on what you know now, as well as its past performance.

Dollar-Cost Averaging

What happens if you buy a stock that subsequently crashes? This happens to the very best of us. If this happened to you, don't get depressed. Don't think that you suck at investing. Don't think that all is lost. If you get caught in a downturn, it might be an amazing opportunity.

Now, it's important to note that almost all stocks experience a pullback. I have yet to come across a stock that has appreciated positively with no dips in its trading history. I'm not aware of a stock that hasn't experienced a day-to-day dip in pricing. All stocks experience a pullback. Even stocks that are well on their way to becoming breakthrough or high-valued stocks will experience dips.

What happens if you bought a stock that drops in value tremendously? Well, you have two options at this point. You can wait for the stock to keep going up and then start buying some more. You're taking bets on its recovery.

The better approach would be to use this as an opportunity. For example, if you bought, for the sake of simplicity, one share of stock at $100 a share, and the price crashes 50% to $50 a share, you can buy one share at $50, and this would average out your holdings to $75 per share.

Ideally, you should wait for the stock to drop so much and then buy a whole lot. This enables you to set your break-even point at a much lower level. For example, using the same hypothetical facts mentioned above, instead of

157

buying one share, you buy 9 shares at $50. So, what happens is, the average price per share gets reduced to $55.

Even if the depressed stock manages to limp along and possibly pop up here and there, it doesn't have to pop up all that much to get all your money back from your position because once it hits $55, you're at break-even territory. Compare this with breaking even at $75 or, worse yet, waiting for the stock to come back to $100 a share. It's anybody's guess whether it will back to that level.

This strategy is called dollar-cost averaging, and it is very useful. You must have free cash available, and you must use that free cash at the right time.

That's how you maximize its value. That's how you fully take advantage of opportunities that present themselves. Otherwise, you might be in a situation where the stock crashes so hard that you could have broken even very easily with little money spent, but unfortunately, you were locked out because you don't have the cash to do it.

Buy Self Liquidating Assets

Another investing strategy you can take is to buy assets that pay for themselves. For example, if you spent a million dollars buying a building, but the building generates rents totaling $100,000 per year, the building pays for itself in roughly 13 years or more, factoring in taxes and other costs.

Self-liquidating assets may seem too good to be true, but they are very real. Most of this applies to certain types of real estate, like commercial properties. However, this strategy also applies to stocks and bonds.

For example, if you buy stocks that have no dividend and you buy bonds, you can use the bond interest to start paying off your stock's portfolio. Of course, this can take quite a bit of time if you factor in interest rates as well as taxes.

Smart Money Valuation

Another winning strategy is to buy into private corporations as a sophisticated investor at a much lower valuation. Now keep in mind that many mobile app companies are popping up all over the United States. You don't necessarily have to live in Silicon Valley of California to have access to these types of companies.

The great thing about these companies is that in the beginning, they require very little capital. Many require "Angel," "per-Angel," or even raw seed capital. The founder would have a rough idea of software, an app, or a website. This is the most basic stage of a company's evolution.

Now, when you come in as a source of seed capital, you can lock into a large chunk of the company's stock for a very low valuation. For example, somebody comes up with a startup idea, and the initial cost is a maximum of $1 million. If you were to invest $250,000, you have a 25% stake in the company.

You may be thinking that 25% of a company that's not worth that much, which is very, very risky, doesn't seem like a winning proposition. Well, keep in mind that after the seed stage, the company's valuation usually goes up. So, once your money has been used to push the company further along its developmental path, the company's valuation starts to go up, especially if they now have something more concrete to show other investors.

You may be asking yourself, okay, the smart money valuation thing sounds awesome. This is great in theory, but is it real? How can the Average Joe investor get in on such deals?

There are websites like Angel List and others, as well as LinkedIn groups that publicize startup projects that are actively recruiting investors. Of course, you need to do your homework and pay attention to the track record of the founders.

Chapter 13.   How to Use Both Macroeconomic and Microeconomic Analysis

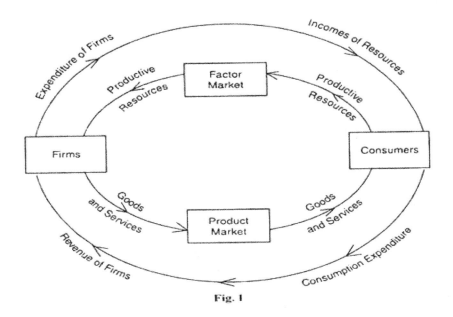

Fig. 1

163

You can't go to war without a weapon. You can't just buy a stock; you must do extensive research. You must learn to be your own stock analyst. This will help you make wise and sound investment decisions.

To do comprehensive stock research, you must apply two methods used in economics—microeconomics analysis and macroeconomic analysis.

Macro-Economic Analysis

As discussed earlier in this book, economic forces (such as the law of supply and demand) affect stock prices. So, before you invest in a stock, you have to use a top-down global research approach. You must look at the global trends. You must look at the big picture.

As of this writing, Airbnb is not a public company yet, but for the purpose of discussion, let's assume that it is. A lot of cities in Europe and in the United States have banned Airbnb, but it continues to grow in various cities in the world. In fact, you can find a lot of great Airbnb deals in Bali, Malaysia, Singapore, Zurich, Mykonos, and Faro. Plus, it still has a number of untapped markets. If you look at the big picture, you'll see that Airbnb is still a great investment because of its huge growth potential.

Aside from looking at the company's global overview, you must also consider other factors, such as:

Interest Rates

When the interest rate is high, it would be more costly for companies and individuals to pay their debts. This decreases their disposable income and their spending. This also affects business revenues and can drive down the stock prices.

But, when a country has a low-interest rate, people have more disposable income. They'll end up buying more stuff. This could lead to an increase in stock prices.

However, you have to take note that rising interest rates can benefit specific industries, such as the financial sector — banks, mortgage companies, lending companies, and insurance companies.

The Cyclical Nature of an Industry

Before you buy a company's stock, you have to determine if that company belongs to a cyclical industry.

Cyclical sectors such as the automobile industry and the construction industry are sensitive to the ups and downs of the economy. When the economy is good, their prices go up, but they go down when there's a recession.

Try to avoid investing in companies in cyclical sectors (unless you're very good at timing your investments). You'd want to invest in a stock that can withstand economic setbacks.

Stock Market Index

As previously discussed, an index tracks the performance of market leaders. So, in essence, it reflects the overall health of the stock market. If an index is trending up, it means that stock market players are a bit optimistic and a bull market may be happening.

Industry-Wide Research

Let's say that you want to invest in luxury brands such as Louis Vuitton (LVMH) or YSL. Before you do that, you must look into the overall health of that industry.

If you look closely, you might discover that luxury brands are not doing as well as they used to be because of online shops and China-made products.

Micro- Economic Analysis

When you do macro-economic analysis, you are looking at the economy and the industry, but understand that microeconomic analysis uses a "bottom-up" approach. This means that you have to do extensive company research.

You have to look into the different aspects of the company, such as:

- **The Company's Product** — Is the product good? Does it have loyal customers? Is the product going to be relevant ten years from now? Let's say that a music store is selling its stocks. Would you buy it? Well, let's face it: no one buys CDs anymore. We just download music from the internet or check YouTube. Technology is changing by the minute. A widely used product may become irrelevant and unnecessary in the next few years. Just look at what happened to diskettes.

- **Sales and Revenue** — Are the company earning money? Are their products doing well in the market?

- **Debt to Equity Ratio** — Is the company's debt bigger than its equity? If so, then you should run as fast as you can.

- **P/E Ratio** — If the company has a high P/E ratio, it means that it has high growth potential. However, it also means that the stock is overvalued. A low P/E ratio means that the company has low growth potential, but it also means that it's overvalued. If you're into growth investing, choose a company with a high P/E ratio. But you have to choose a company with a low P/E ratio if you're into value investing.

- **Earnings per Share (EPS)** — A company with high EPS is really doing well. It's profitable. So, assuming other factors check out (e.g. it's not using a lot of unsustainable debt to generate the earnings), it's a good idea to invest in a company with a high EPS.

- **Company Management** — Do you trust the people managing the company? Do they engage in unethical business practices? If you don't trust the people running the company, then avoid it at all costs.

Also, make sure that the company's profit has been trending upward at least in the last five years.

Chapter 14.   How to Create a

Secure Financial Future

In today's scenario, where the economy hides and seeks some sort of position, financial security is a must for every individual. Although it is a broad category, financial security, however, means investment and income in the future. Look at the market, and you'll find different options for investment. Often it's hard to pick the right option.

Trading is yet another investment opportunity that offers no limits, unlike other investment strategies, but just good returns. However, as we all know, the stock market is a constantly changing environment, and we need technical analysis to learn from it; that will ensure your market success.

Unfortunately, many of us are not going to analyze it and continue to invest. The result is obvious, and that is why people often do not respond disproportionately to stock trading.

On the other hand, many of us profit from the same market, but attitudes and strategies differ. Why is one person a successful trader and another failing trader? If you know the difference in this small line, your investment strategy is guaranteed to succeed. Before you start trading, there are many things to consider:

- **Financial Strength** — Firstly, your financial strength — how much you want to invest — must be analyzed. You can start with small funds if you are a new trader. You can add more funds to your investment plan once you make money.

- **Experts in Finance** — investment is not a simple task. Proper planning is, therefore, a must. If you know market trends and trading experience, you can plan without assistance. However, if you are new and would like some assistance, please consult financial experts — they are available online and offer the best investment plan.

- **Comprehensive Market Knowledge** — A successful trader needs good market knowledge.

- **Online Stock Broke** — Because we are unable to trade directly, your broker makes all forms of trading and charges a small fee in return. It's like a connection between the trader and the stock market.

You should therefore have a good broker who can also give you advice and let you know about the most profitable company shares.

- **Technical Analysis** — A complete competitive market analysis is a must. You have to analyze stock price trends in the last 3 to 5 days, and you can predict market mood further. This research, however, does not always succeed; it still gives us an idea of the market.

- **Positive Attitude** — it is not your attitude; it is your business attitude. Those who often see the market as a risky forum affect many of us and create a negative business attitude. In that very case, you can make the wrong decision, even if you are on the right track. Therefore, you must be optimistic and try to believe in yourself.

One of the main factors for successful trading is the ability to understand the market and to adapt to changing circumstances. Once you get to know the market moods, you can better reap the advantages. Invest now and build a strong future financial reserve.

How to Choose the Right Stocks to Invest In

Mia worked in a software development company for fifteen years. She's good at her job, but she was always stressed and tired. So, she decided to give stock market investment a try in order to build a passive income portfolio that would help her retire early. She met with an old friend named Kate, a financial analyst. Kate helped her invest in high-quality and fast-growing stocks.

After two years, Mia had earned $650,000 capital appreciation profit. She quit her job and traveled around the world. She soon used part of her earnings to establish her own graphic design company. Her $650,000 grew to over $2 million.

Mia is living her dream life. She owns her time. She has a successful business, and she even bought a beach house in Miami.

Chloe was Mia's former colleague. Like Mia, she's been working in the software development industry for about fifteen years. She was also tired. After she heard about Mia's success, she decided to invest in stocks, too.

Chloe didn't know anything about the stock market and didn't know how to choose the right stocks. She invested in companies that were buried in debt and engaged in unethical business practices. So, she ended up losing $10,000.

A lot of people get rich through stock market investment, but many people lose huge amounts of money too. This is the reason why you should be careful in choosing the right stocks to invest in. You have to be clear about your investment goals and use the right strategies that work for you and match your risk tolerance level. You must also do extensive research before you place your bet on a stock.

Setting an Investment Objective

Before you start investing, you should be clear about what your investment objectives are. You should also decide what type of investor you want to be. Do you want to be a long-term investor? Or, do you want to be a day trader, trading stocks by the minute?

You must be clear about what you want to achieve through stock market investing. How much are you willing to invest? How much do you want to earn each year? What are you willing to risk?

You need to set financial goals like how much you want to earn in one year or in five years. You should also set non-financial goals. Why? Well, your investment earnings are just mere tools that you can use to support your non-financial goals. So, what do you want to achieve? Do you want to have a grand wedding? Do you want to travel to a foreign country at least twice a year?

Factors to Consider in Choosing a Stock

The key to building a profitable investment portfolio is choosing the right stocks. When you're starting, buying individual stocks is costlier than investing in low-cost mutual funds. Below are the factors that you should consider in choosing stocks to invest in.

- **Growth in Earnings**

  Before you invest in a company, you should check its earnings and make sure that it's consistently growing over time. The growth doesn't have to be huge. You just have to look for an upward trend in earnings.

  For example, let's say that you have an extra $3,000 and you want to invest it in stock. You're looking to invest in two companies. Company A is one of the biggest steel manufacturers in the country, while Company B produces the nation's best-selling batteries.

  Take time to examine the data below:

  - **Company A: Leading Steel Manufacturer**

Year	Earnings

2005	$2,158,111,202
2006	$2,160,369,000
2007	$2,080,250,000
2008	$1,988,910,000
2009	$1,888,630,121
2010	$1,780,980,011
2011	$1,761,918,870

2012	$1,709,919,450
2013	$1,670,980,689
2014	$1,659,658,905
2015	$1,640,050,814
2016	$1,590,010,110
2017	$1,550,000,289
2018	$1,499,110,980

o **Company B: Leading Battery Manufacturer**

Year	Earnings
2005	$750,000,905
2006	$805,963,960
2007	$815,750,690
2008	$909,530,066
2009	$915,784,210
2010	$918,974,560

2011	$990,741,632
2012	$1,101,890,390
2013	$1,156,120,450
2014	$1,190,110,000
2015	$1,220,000,980
2016	$1,240,780,360
2017	$1,310,000.550

2018	$1,399,222,080

If you look closely, you'll see that Company A has a lot more earnings than Company B. However, its revenue has been declining since 2008. This means that the company is facing problems. It could be mismanagement or a decreasing market share due to an aggressive competitor entering the space.

 Company B, on the other hand, has had steady growing earnings since 2006. This company is doing something right and is more worthy of your hard-earned money.

- **Stability**

Sir Tim Berners-Lee published a paper about a proposed information management program called the "internet" in 1989. He then implemented the first successful communication between a Hypertext Transfer Protocol (HTTP) and a server a few months later.

In 1990, Berners-Lee began writing the World Wide Web (www) — the first-ever web browser. The next year, he launched the first-ever web page. This forever changed the world. This is what stock market players call a black swan.

According to risk analyst Nassim Nicholas Taleb, a black swan is an event that's hard to predict that can forever change the world. And if you're wise enough to predict or at least spot a black swan at its early stage, you're going to win big in the stock market and in business. This explains why early internet entrepreneurs like Jack Ma and Jeff Bezos are extremely wealthy.

And soon, promising internet companies decided to go public and the investors went crazy placing their eggs in the "internet business basket."

But after the tech industry got a little too crowded and the world experienced a stock market crash in 2008, the revenues of internet companies became volatile. So, a lot of investors ended up losing huge amounts of money.

Even so, this is just an example. It doesn't mean that you shouldn't invest in the tech industry. All companies are bound to lose their stock value at some point, especially during periods of recession and economic crisis.

To achieve long-term success in the stock market, you have to invest in companies that are strong and stable enough to endure unfavorable economic conditions. Erratic stock price fluctuation is not a good sign.

To illustrate this point, look at the graph below:

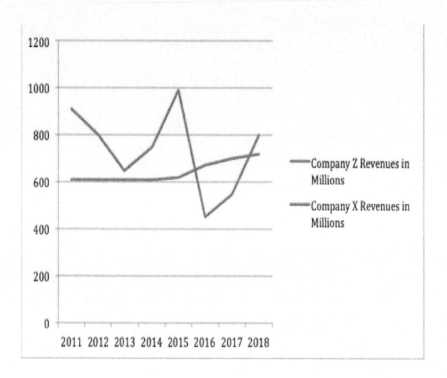

Notice that Company Z's revenue doesn't fluctuate as much as Company X's. This means that it's more stable and a good choice for long-term investment.

Chapter 15.   Stock Market Strategies for Profitable Investing

Learning how to use successful bond market strategies will vary between the loss and possible profits of all your hard-earned money. These tips help you find the right investment strategies to use and avoid those that harm you more.

The Business Know

It is necessary to know the market before you can begin investment so that you can better understand how to use effective stock market strategies. Study the market as best as you can, including those stocks that are of interest to you — there are plenty of websites and other reference material that can help you get an understanding of the market.

Besides, partnering with a reputable financial advisor or creditable financial information provider is a perfect stock market strategy to understand better the market and what it can do for you.

Evite Fraud

Beginners are particularly vulnerable to fraud and schemes designed to draw prospective investors to divide their hard-playing cash. Many who fall for these sly stock market schemes won't do anything; in fact, only the scammers themselves profit from these scams!

The bottom line — most definitely if it sounds too good to be true. Equipped with the right investment strategies and expertise, you won't fall into these enticing schemes.

A Stock Broker Notice

An investment plan is a perfect way to use a stockbroker as a reliable broker will help you to decide on your portfolio and help you pick the right stock for your situation. A trustworthy broker can use his expertise to help you gain greater market knowledge, including trends, stock growth, and whether to buy or sell.

Furthermore, a stockbroker can show you even better investment strategies than you can buy. A reliable broker will happily assist you with your investments and will do everything possible to lead you in the right direction.

Learning how to play the stock market can be terrifying for beginning investors in particular. By learning about the market, avoiding schemes that are too good for you to be true, and finding a reputable stockbroker, you will learn successful stock market strategies to make your investment profitable.

It is crucial for beginners to have a solid understanding of the market and how to be as effective as possible before even beginning to invest in the stock market. The following bonds will lead you in the right direction.

Train Yourself

The first step towards being a good investor is to educate you. Take a few lessons in accounting, read as many books on investment as possible, and look online for different facets of the business and how it works for you.

Another suggestion that helps you become a better investor is to talk to a licensed stockbroker or financial advisor. A renowned advisor can provide you with direct personal information which you are not able to find in books or posts, and can also sit one-on-one with you and answer all your questions.

Take Stock Exchange Tools

Another smart tip is to use apps for some tasks. It is advisable to invest in personal finance software that can help you handle your money and track income and losses. A program that helps you monitor your stock market portfolio and trace when to buy or sell will be another software to consider; evaluate potential profits vs. risks of a specific stock, and track stock prices.

Continue to Train

One of the best investment tips, particularly for beginners, is to continue to practice until you have a good understanding of the market and its concepts. If you do not follow some other bond suggestion, it should certainly be a priority, regardless of what.

Many stock simulation programs, without taking risks and investing, will make you experience the real thing. Some of these systems are more practical than others, but all of them help you understand the idea of stock purchasing and trading.

This quick, productive tip lets you learn how to play the market and how to make it work for you. There are many stock trading tips, particularly for beginners, but you can only hope to make the most out of investing through knowledge and experience. The tips listed here are designed to help beginners learn about the market and make the best choices to succeed.

Chapter 16.   COVID-19 Effects on Working with Stocks

The stock market's reaction to the COVID-19 pandemic and the subsequent economic fallout has raised both fears and questions. This column delves into unexpected developments. There is evidence that shareholders favored the less distressed companies, and that credit facilities and government guarantees, lower policy interest rates, and stock price lockdowns helped to minimize the stock price decline. Fundamentals, on the other hand, only account for a limited portion of stock market fluctuations at the country level. Overall, it's difficult to argue that the correlations between stock prices and fundamentals have been shaky at best.

The World Health Organization (WHO) declared on June 8, 2020, that the COVID-19 pandemic was worsening around the world and cautioned against complacency: "the majority of people worldwide are still vulnerable to infection. "...With more than six months left in the pandemic, now is not the time for any nation to ease up on the gas." The US stock market started its fourth consecutive week of gains on the same day. The S&amp P 500 index has returned to where it was at the start of 2020, erasing the historical decline (one-third of its value) that occurred between February 20 and March 23, 2020, as if nothing had happened. As seen in the graph, this is absolutely unparalleled.

Is there something unusual about the stock market behavior during COVID-19? The reaction of financial markets poses serious concerns as the world suffers from the worst economic crisis since the Great Depression (Baldwin and Weder di Mauro 2020a, 2020b, Bénassy-Quéré and Weder di Mauro 2020, Coibon et al. 2020). Stock prices have been wildly fluctuating since the start of the crisis. They dismissed the pandemic at first, then panicked as it spread to Europe. They are now acting as if the millions of people who have been poisoned, the 400,000 deaths, and the containment of half the world's population has had no economic effects.

Paul Krugman (2020) said out loud what many people were thinking in one of his famous New York Times columns: "Whenever you consider the economic ramifications of stock prices, you want to remember three rules." To begin with, the stock market is not the same as the economy.

Second, the stock market isn't the same thing as the economy. Third, the stock market is not a replacement for the economy (...). The correlation between stock performance and real economic growth, which is largely driven by the oscillation between greed and fear, has always been shaky at best. "Malkiel and Shiller (2020)," two other well-known economists, have also discussed the stock market's strange conduct in the face of the pandemic. The suspected stock market irrationality, according to Malkiel, is just "apparent," and the COVID-19 crisis does not "imply that markets are dysfunctional" since there are no arbitrage possibilities and stock markets remain difficult to beat. "Speculative prices can statistically mimic a random walk, but they are not as bound to genuine knowledge (...), says Shiller. The infectious stories about the coronavirus had their own internal complexities that were only tangentially linked to the truth."

What lessons can be learned about stock market actions from the COVID-19 crisis? This debate is particularly important for financial economists, but it is also important because the general public has a negative perception of

stock markets, which should worry us (Rajan 2015) —
especially after the COVID-19 crisis placed science and
'experts' to the test (Aksoy et al. 2020), without sparing
economists.

A rapidly growing body of research looking at stock market
reactions to the COVID-19 pandemic is already providing
some insights. Although the stock market's actions during
the pandemic could seem spontaneous, irrational, or even
insane at first glance, closer observation shows that they
did not respond randomly. Several studies have shown that
stock markets are effective at discounting the most
vulnerable companies: those that are financially fragile,
vulnerable to international value chain disruption,
vulnerable to corporate social responsibility, or less resilient
to social distancing (Alburque et al. 2020, Ding et al. 2020,
Fahlenbrach et al. 2020, Pagano et al. 2020, Ramelli and
Wagner 2020). Furthermore, it appears that, at least in the
medium term, stock market declines are linked to analyst
forecast revisions (Landier and Thesmar 2020). We
approach these papers from a macroeconomic standpoint.

While the studies described above provide useful details, some questions remain unanswered.

What has been the response of the stock market to the COVID-19 pandemic? How do we understand the disparities in responses around countries? Are there any macroeconomic or institutional factors that influence stock market response across countries, and if so, which ones? Are these disparities the product of how governments treated the pandemic? How have financial markets responded to nationwide lockdowns and economic policies aimed at 'flattening' the curves of infection and recession? (2020 Gourinchas)

We discuss how stock markets have incorporated public knowledge about the COVID-19 pandemic and subsequent lockdowns in our recent paper (Capelle-Blancard and Desroziers 2020). Despite the fact that the COVID-19 shock was global, not all countries were affected in the same way, and they did not react in the same way. This high heterogeneity is something we take advantage of. We want to understand the differences in stock market responses by looking at the situation in each country prior to the crisis, as well as the subsequent containment measures (social distancing and stay-at-home orders) and economic policies (fiscal and monetary) that were introduced during the crisis. From January to April 2020, we consider a panel of 74 nations, which can be divided into four phases: incubation, outbreak, fear, and rebound. We gathered regular data on stock index prices, COVID-19 total cases and deaths, global market sentiment and volatility, government responses to the outbreak, and various indicators of mobility for each region (or lack thereof).

Three main results emerge about stock market reactions during the COVID-19 pandemic. First, after initially ignoring the pandemic (until February 21, 2020), financial markets responded strongly to the rise in the number of infected people in each country (February 23 to March 20, 2020), with volatility increasing as fears about the pandemic increased. Following central bank intervention (23 March to 20 April 2020), however, news of the health crisis no longer seemed to bother shareholders, and shares rebounded all over the world. Second, it appears that country-specific characteristics had little, if any, impact on stock market responses. Stock markets in countries more vulnerable to the pandemic did not respond as strongly, either because of systemic economic fragility (for example, indebted countries) or because of exposure to transmission vectors (for example, countries with 'at-risk' populations). Third, the number of COVID-19 cases in neighboring (but mostly wealthy) countries piqued investors' interest. Fourth, the fall in stock prices was mitigated by credit facilities and government guarantees, lower policy interest rates, and lockout measures.

Finally, do capital markets take into account all available information? In fact, we can see the glass as either half-full or half-empty. On the one hand, the stock market's behavior during the COVID-19 pandemic is not entirely coincidental. Our research indicates that the reaction of stock markets was affected by health policies introduced during the crisis to restrict virus transmission and macroeconomic policies aimed at supporting businesses, rather than the situation of countries prior to the crisis. Fundamentals, on the other hand, only account for a (very) small portion of stock market volatility. It's difficult to deny that the connection between stock prices and fundamentals has been anything but loose, as Krugman and Shiller have claimed.

Conclusion

There are also many different types of investments, orders, and such that the individual may make. It is crucial that the investor knows the differences between these and can decide on which methods the investor wishes to invest in. However, the investor must know the pros and cons of each to reach that conclusion. The investor must educate himself or herself before making any further decisions on their investments and strategies for trading. There are many elements of the stock market that one must familiarize themselves with; the more that you know, the better the chance of you receiving a high return on your investment is.

Stock market investing can be very powerful for any person looking to create wealth or build a side income. Among all the asset classes, stock investments have generated the best returns historically. Consequently, it is beneficial for you over the long term that you develop a sound understanding of this highly profitable investment avenue.

The next step is to follow this through and begin your quest as a stock investor. It is important to begin by setting goals for yourself as an investor. You must consider all of the variables involved in investing. Setting goals will help provide you with a sense of direction. By using this as a reference, you may decide on which path of investing you will choose. What will be the time period of your investment? Will you purchase individual stocks or ETFs? How much risk are you willing to take in your investments? These questions, among others, must be answered to provide you with clear goals in your investing. After this, you may create an account, fund your account, and start trading. There must be research done, and you must select your stocks. After this, you are on the path to success in trading.

After you have accomplished this, you must continue to conduct research on the market, monitor your stocks, and manage your portfolio. Being an investor is an ongoing process. This can really help you to get started in learning about stock, and it may serve as a reference guide throughout your stock investing career. There will constantly be changes in the economy, the stock market will fluctuate every day, and the stocks themselves will continuously move. However, the basic concepts of stock will always be helpful to know, and this provides its readers with those basics that are necessary for one to be successful in stock investing.

The goal is to help investors, especially those who are just getting started with investing in the stock market, to learn the basic concepts of the stock market that will help them to initiate the trading process and become both successful and profitable in their investments.

Stock investing requires discipline, patience, and thoughtful analysis. Diversification is an essential strategy for successful stock investing. Keeping your emotions in check is also a crucial part of becoming a successful investor. A long-term approach to stock investments provides many times good returns.

By reading it to the end, you are proving that you are disciplined and ready to work hard! Many rookie investors spend their money investing blindly. Unlike the majority, you have taken your time to acquire knowledge to make wise decisions. Good job!

Printed in Great Britain
by Amazon